WATERSIDE PUBS

Also by Ronald Russell

Lost Canals of England and Wales

Ronald Russell

WATERSIDE PUBS
Pubs of the Inland Waterways

DAVID & CHARLES

Newton Abbot London North Pomfret (VT) Vancouver

For Jill

ISBN 0 7153 6743 9

Library of Congress Catalog Card Number

74-81057

© RONALD RUSSELL 1974

Set in 11 on 13pt Garamond and printed in
Great Britain by Latimer Trend & Company Ltd Plymouth
for David & Charles (Holdings) Limited
South Devon House Newton Abbot Devon

Published in the United States of America
by David & Charles Inc
North Pomfret Vermont 05053 USA

Published in Canada
by Douglas David & Charles Limited
3645 McKechnie Drive West Vancouver BC

CONTENTS

LIST OF ILLUSTRATIONS

Drawings by Robert Cox

INTRODUCTION

~~~~~~

There are more than 70,000 licensed houses in England and Wales. How many of them are waterside no one really knows. An answer, if it were possible to give one, would depend on definition—how near the water is 'waterside'? For the purposes of this book I have taken it to mean 'within a few yards', and left it at that. And, to anticipate a query about 'water', I have considered only the navigable waterways, the rivers, canals and Broads which were once the trading routes of the country. For the waterside pub, in its humbler way, was the equivalent of the coaching inn, those great houses on the main routes radiating from London where horses were baited or changed and travellers refreshed or lodged for the night. On coaching inns many books have been written; on waterside pubs, very few.

At a guess, there would be something approaching 2,000 pubs alongside navigable waterways. The range is wide, from the glossy Thames-side hotels to the Victorian boatman's beerhouse. Some descend from religious foundations; hospices by bridge crossings where pilgrims found food and rest. Some were ferry houses; others were converted from wharfside offices. Farmers finding canals being cut through their property turned the occasion to advantage by selling their home-brewed beer direct to the labourers—the navvies—and then to the boatmen; sometimes the sideline became profitable and the farms were changed into pubs. There are, of course, far fewer waterside pubs than there were in

The *Hartley Arms*, Wheaton Aston, Shropshire Union Canal

the days of commercial waterborne traffic. On some busy stretches of canal there could be between five and ten pubs in a single mile, while the average frequency now is about three miles for every pub. The remarkable increase in pleasure cruising in the last few years, however, has halted the decline and there are some instances of pubs re-opening after years of closure.

The war, slum clearance, new road schemes, increasing demands for office accommodation, redevelopment of waterside premises— these are other reasons for the disappearance of very many licensed houses. Norwich, although never a major port, used to have a busy waterside area and the names of the pubs, almost all of which have gone, reflected the various activities. There was the

Norwich a Port, recalling a catch phrase of the early nineteenth century, and the *Steam Packet*, remembering the vessel that took passengers on outings to Bemerton and Coldham Hall down the River Yare. In King Street there was the *Waterman*, whose landlord at one time also doubled as a barber and placed a sign over the entrance which read:

> Roam not from pole to pole but step in here
> Where naught excels the shaving but the beer.

In the same street the two types of sailing craft on which the prosperity of the region depended were recalled in the name of the *Keel & Wherry*, the keels being replaced by wherries in the nineteenth century. The *Old Barge* is a pub no more; it dated from before 1600 and is said to have been the house of Roger Medday. who was bailiff of Norwich when Edward III was king. The *Cinder Ovens* closed about the end of World War I; the name of this house came from the coke ovens or furnaces at the back of the building, built into the base of the boom tower at Carrow bridge. By Bishop's bridge was the *Red Lion*, once owned by James Hobrough, head of a firm which had much to do with lightering, dredging and piling on the local waterways. The *Red Lion* used to have two flagpoles with a wherry vane on top of each. There was a *New Star* on Quayside, and the *General Windham* where the Pockthorpe Guild held its annual dumpling dinners. There were also two pubs called the *Adam & Eve*, one of which survives. This one is a very old house, parts of the building possibly dating back to the foundation of the nearby Great Hospital in 1249. It is tucked into a quiet corner near the cathedral, close to the Wensum. Despite some updating, it retains its pattern of several small rooms on different levels. The *Adam & Eve* was a beerhouse until recently and used to be popular with watermen. One landlady, Mrs Howes, owned a wherry which she named after the pub; the wherry was employed in bringing sea sand from Gorleston to spread on the floors of houses. The other *Adam & Eve* was not a waterside house but is worth mentioning because it is said to have once been kept by a landlord named Cain Abel.

The Norwich story can be paralleled in many other cities and towns which derived their initial prosperity from being situated on a navigable river. There are also the towns which owed their prosperity to a canal that, when trade declined, was legally abandoned and then filled in. A study of Victorian directories reveals the enormous number of licensed houses with addresses such as Canal Row, Canal Terrace, Canal Parade in towns like Cardiff and Newport where over half a million tons of coal and iron used to arrive by canal in the busy years of the mid-nineteenth century. The beerhouses and taverns have almost all gone; only here and there a more substantial inn remains, Packet Boat hotel or something similar, where in the past passengers spent an occasional night.

There is another side to the picture. With the great increase in private car ownership it became clear that many waterside pubs, which had lost their original purpose with the decline of water-borne trade, might with profit be developed to attract the car customer, the river or canal providing a magnet. Stables were levelled to provide space for car-parking and toilets; lounges with riverside windows were built on. Divisions between small rooms were removed and large bars installed from behind which the tenant or manager could be properly monarch of all he surveyed. Walls sprouted pictures of vintage cars; horse-brass factories in Birmingham worked overtime. Juke boxes were installed so that no customer could engage in quiet conversation with another. Chrome replaced brass and plastic replaced wood. Chickens died in thousands, to be dismembered and put into baskets, tons of crenellated chips were ferried across from Canada, and for the succulent scampi the seas were scoured. From among the bottles the brewers' advertisements twinkled and shone, so that at least you could not be ignorant as to who was responsible for the decor or the beer you consumed.

It would be grossly unfair to suggest that all public house renovation is tasteless or maladroit. In some houses tact, in others imagination, have come into play, and in most instances what is there now is at least cleaner and more comfortable than what was there before. In a few canalside houses the canal itself has provided inspiration. There are reminders of the past in the shape of pictures, models, painted ware—not just produced for the occasion, but the genuine article preserved where otherwise it might have been lost or thrown away. Some riverside ferry houses have memorials of the ferries in their years of operation; lists of ferry-men, details of charges, legal documents. But these memorials are to be found more often in houses which the hand of modernisation has touched only lightly, not with that imperious gesture which sweeps all the past away. Why does one so often hear the word 'unspoiled' when people talk about the pubs they really like?

Recent years have seen the amalgamation of many large breweries and the taking over of many smaller ones. This, of course, is a continuous process; many of the pubs referred to in this book brewed their own beer at first and many of them have passed through the hands of half a dozen different breweries before reaching their present owners. But it does mean that there is progressively a smaller variety of beers available and beer drawn straight from the barrel is becoming difficult to find. To pontificate about taste in this matter is unwise; one man's nectar is another man's swipes. Hence in the following chapters there are very few references to beer. Pub coffee, on the other hand, is nearly always good. It is a pity that more pubs do not serve it.

One unfortunate result of the transference of pubs from one ownership to another is that their present owners frequently have no information as to the history of their houses. It is the history of the pubs, especially in relation to the history of the waterways by which they stand, that is the main concern of this book. There are some knowledgeable landlords, more generally in free houses, and local historians do sometimes frequent their local pubs. Often, however, information is hard to come by. The files of Record Offices have little or nothing to disclose; likewise with Public Libraries and the offices of the local newspaper. There is little information because there has been little to record save changes of ownership or name. There may be an oral tradition, living on in the memories of the older frequenters, and sometimes one is fortunate enough to discover something of this. But with the more mobile society of the mid-twentieth century this oral tradition is weakening; the best of it has already gone. Fewer and fewer remember the waterways in their trading years. Never well documented, this aspect of the past is slipping away. We know the names of the canal company committees, the river engineers, the

movements of the shares, the statistics of freight carried. What we
know too little about is the detail of the lives of those who worked
the boats and used these waterside pubs. In this respect the pub
that has survived with little alteration is especially valuable to the
social historian. This is what makes houses like the *Bird in Hand*
at Kent Green, the *Anchor* at High Offley, the *Ship* at the head of
Levington Creek so precious today. They may be short of
'facilities' or 'amenities', but what they do have is of far greater
value; a sense of the past enduring into the present, a past that is
still alive. They tell us more than books.

The waterways themselves are used as guides to the pubs which
I refer to. In the time available, to cover every waterway and every
pub was not possible. There are some obvious omissions; the
Llangollen Canal, for instance, some of the commercial waterways
in the north-east, and the south coast rivers. I was too late for the
Neptune Hotel, alongside the abandoned Rochdale Canal at Hebden
Bridge, which was built to serve the canal and closed a year ago.
Certain pubs I regret not having visited; the isolated *Pyewipe* on the
Fossdyke, the *Anchor* at Johnson's Hillock—a favourite of Charles
Hadfield, canal historian *in principio*—some of the dockside pubs in
Goole, and, in particular, the *Engine Inn* at Cark-in-Cartmel. This
stands near the River Eea, to which I can find no reference in
waterway history. The landlord writes that it was built in 1689
and has never been altered structurally since. Apparently barges
used to offload coal and take on cotton from Lancashire's first
cotton mill on the opposite bank of the river. The inn, once called
the *Fire Engine*, was an old post house and the stables still exist. It
sounds fascinating; perhaps there will be an opportunity to include
this and the others in a second volume. Those who are interested
in the waterways administered by British Waterways Board will
find comprehensive lists of the pubs alongside them in the recently
published Nicholson's Guides, and of many rivers there are charts
available which indicate the public houses.

Omission from these pages implies nothing, nor should inference
be drawn from inclusion. Any points of view expressed are personal only. But I hope many would agree that in the hectic years
of the 1970s it is remarkable that, for the cost of a few pence, you
can still obtain rest, refreshment, and usually warmth with a

degree of comfort, in the house of a stranger—a Public House. There may be times when one is tempted to agree with Viscount Torrington who, after one unfortunate experience, wrote that he looked upon an inn 'as the seat of all roguery, profaneness, and debauchery . . . the innkeepers are insolent, the hostlers are sulky, the chambermaids are pert, and the waiters are impertinent; the meat is tough, the wine is foul, the beer is hard, the sheets are wet, the linnen is dirty and the knives are never clean'd.' But most of us, I hope, would in general concur with what Dr Johnson said in 1776. It has been often quoted since, but I make no excuse for quoting it again: 'There is nothing which has yet been contrived by man, by which so much happiness has been produced, as by a good tavern or inn.'

2

RIVERSIDE 1
London to Northampton

∞∞∞∞∞∞∞∞∞∞∞∞∞∞∞∞∞∞∞∞∞∞∞∞∞∞∞∞∞∞∞∞

The Lee, from Bow Creek to Hertford, is one of the oldest of navigations. Well over 500 years ago legislation was passed to improve its condition; since then, in Priestley's* words, it 'has afforded a cheap and ready transit for corn, malt, wool and other agricultural produce to the metropolis; and in return, of coal, timber, deals, bricks, paving-stones, groceries, cloth, and various articles of daily consumption'. For centuries it has also provided London with a large measure of its water supply. And it has also served, and still serves, Londoners as a water playground. Anglers, boaters, picnickers, cyclists escape the city and the suburbs to refresh themselves by the river, to such an extent that the Lee Valley Regional Park has been established to supplement Nature which, it may be admitted, Man has not always dealt kindly with in this area.

The Lee pubs reflect the river's many functions. The late

---

* Joseph Priestley, *Historical Account of the Navigable Rivers, Canals, and Railways, throughout Great Britain*, 1831 (reprinted 1969, David & Charles).

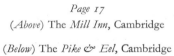

Page 17

(*Above*) The *Mill Inn*, Cambridge

(*Below*) The *Pike & Eel*, Cambridge

Page 18

(*Above*) The *Ferry Boat Inn*, Holywell, on the Great Ouse

(*Below*) The *Cutter*, Ely

Victorian *King's Head* in Clapton was a boating and picnic centre from 1890 until 1914 and, like many Lee pubs, it contains plenty of stuffed fish. There is still barge traffic on the southern section of the river, timber being the main freight—much of which seems to find its way into the river. Fish do survive, and both the *Prince of Wales*, in Lea Bridge Road, and the *Ferry Boat* at Tottenham are popular with anglers. Near the eighteenth-century *Cook's Ferry Inn* at Edmonton there is likely to be better sport. This is a fine red-brick three-storey house. An aquatint of 1831 shows three top-hatted gentlemen fishing for roach (they appear to have caught one each) observed by two more on the opposite bank, while several others enjoy their drinks outside the pub. The *Cook's Ferry* contrasts with the *Royal Small Arms* by Enfield lock and the maintenance yard, not far from the gate of the Royal Small Arms factory. This nineteenth-century house has an enormous public bar of unbelievable drabness, the only colour being provided by the television set.

An older pub is the *Old English Gentleman* at Waltham Cross. This used to be a farmhouse. It is a small house, rather run-down inside but not unpleasantly so. It must be healthy; the previous landlord held the licence for 57 years. Again, it is popular with anglers as is (what else?) the *Jolly Fisherman* at Stanstead Abbots. So is the equally piscine *Fish & Eels* at Dobbs Weir. Here a water leisure centre is in the making; small boats can be hired and there is civilised parkland in the vicinity. The *Fish & Eels* is about 150 years old, having been extended on the ground floor since first built. There is an attractive jumble of early nineteenth-century bits of roof at the rear. One claim to fame is that the local vicar was its licensee for 4 years during the 1880s. It is still sometimes used by the crews of barges loaded with timber and grain. There is nothing pretentious about the *Fish & Eels*, but there are those who would not say the same about the *Rye House Hotel* at Hoddesdon. This pub was the *King's Arms* in 1756 and for about 100 years after; then it was rebuilt as the *Rye House Hotel*, named after Rye House which stood close by, where a plot was laid to ambush Charles II and James, his son. It didn't work. The gateway of the manor house is all that remains, opposite the pub. This gateway was also bought by the nineteenth-century developer of the pub,

Mr W. H. Teale, who turned the area into pleasure gardens for the less fashionable Londoners. One of the objects they came to see was the Great Bed of Ware, which remained here until 1927. The pub itself is fake Elizabethan, with a Conspirators' Bar and several juke boxes. The surroundings are messy and untidy; but perhaps they will improve.

The riverside at Ware is interesting, with timber and grain wharves and old summerhouses along its banks. Amongst the timber yards is the *Victoria,* which used to be popular with bargemen. It is a Georgian building of some character which at one time in its earlier history is said to have been, improbably, a girls' school. It was certainly a pub in the latter part of the nineteenth century and was kept by a gentleman called Cloggie Saunders before being sold to McMullen's Brewery in 1922. It is worth going to look at the memorial to Sir Hugh Myddleton, originator of the New River in the early seventeeth century, standing on an island in a beautiful tree-clad setting below the church of Great Amwell, about a mile from Ware. The New River, designed to supply London with water from Amwell springs, now takes the water from the Lee.

The head of the Lee navigation is within yards of the *Old Barge* in Hertford, across the river from the bus station. This has been a pub for probably 150 years; the frontage, with its red brick double bay, is Victorian but the interior suggests an older house which has been added to, as does the rear of the building with its black weather-boarding. Attached to the *Old Barge* and alongside the towpath was a row of five cottages, one up one down, their interiors now removed and converted to a hall but looking much as ever outside. On the far side of the small car park was a clay pipe maker's cottage. The *Old Barge* has some interesting old photographs inside and is altogether a pleasant and homely pub.

The River Stort flows into the Lee between Rye House and Dobbs Weir. This is a quiet river, with an occasional lock, an occasional mill and an occasional boat. By Harlow Mill lock is the *Old Mill*; it has lost its works and wheel but the setting is beautiful. There is a reference to a mill hereabouts in Domesday Book, which may refer to this one, although the present building dates only from 1794. In the lounge there is a painting of it functioning as a mill over 100 years ago. It is now a comfortable refuge from the ferocious traffic on A11, with a good restaurant. The Stort navigation ends near Bishop's Stortford railway station and the *Tanners Arms*.

In 1811 there was a survey to determine the line of a canal, to be known as the London & Cambridge Junction, from Bishop's Stortford to the Cam at Clayhithe, a few miles below Cambridge. Three tunnels and fifty-two locks would have to be constructed and the total cost was estimated at over half a million pounds, with a further £45,000 for a branch to Whaddon. But it was possible to raise only one-fifth of the money required and this imaginative but not very practical project was dropped. Had it succeeded there is no doubt that Cambridge could have coped, for the city had been an inland port for centuries—the head of the navigation to King's Lynn. Coal, bricks and timber were being brought by river to Cambridge within the last 50 years. In medieval times where the college gardens now sweep graciously down to the riverside along the Backs there used to be a succession of wharves; then as the colleges were founded and extended their territory so the small wharves disappeared and trade became concentrated on two points; the quayside, by Magdalene College, and King's mill above Silver Street bridge. The construction of Denver Sluice prevented sea-going vessels from reaching Cambridge; protests being unavailing, the town and university combined to seek means of improving the local navigation and in 1702 an Act was passed appointing conservators to regulate and improve the navigation and to collect tolls. The Conservators of the Cam still administer the river.

Some idea of the importance of the river shortly before it began to suffer from railway competition can be gauged from the number of inns and taverns within a few yards of the Common Hithe at Quayside. In 1841 there were over twenty in the short length of Bridge Street, with another five on Quayside itself. Three of these remain: the *Mitre* and the *Baron of Beef*, next to each other, and the *Pickerel* by Magdalene bridge. The oldest part of the *Pickerel* dates from the sixteenth century; it is one of a handful of really old Cambridge inns. The frontage was rebuilt early in the nineteenth century, when a brewery was also built in the yard. Popular with bargemen, who enjoyed watching the cock-fighting in the yard, the *Pickerel*'s reputation was not very salubrious. The Cam and Ouse bargemen, or lightermen, were a tough lot; they had to be, for it was hard work on these rivers especially against the keen winds of the Fens. They were reputed to be the most foul-mouthed in the country, though it is difficult to see how that could be proved. They wore fur caps and sleeved waistcoats made of red or

Victorian Trade Card of the *Pickerel*, Cambridge

blue plush, with glass buttons; they drank deep and, like other Fenmen, were prone to take opium. In a booklet called *The Waterman of the River Cam*, first published in 1825, tracts on 'The Swearer's Prayer' and 'Drunkenness' are referred to. Will Spread, the waterman of the title, having been converted, hung up a little card in the cabin of his house-lighter warning against swearing:

> It chills my blood to hear the blest Supreme,
> Rudely appeal'd to, on each trifling theme;
> Maintain your rank—vulgarity despise,
> To swear is neither brave, polite or wise . . .

Will gave up his old wicked ways and of course 'found in a very short time that his business had increased—that he had now a pound, where before he had not a shilling, and in every sense of the word found himself a Better Man.' So the *Pickerel* lost a customer.

Upstream from Magdalene bridge—the 'Great Bridge' of Cambridge—the river, in summer alive with punts, flows beneath a succession of beautiful bridges linking the colleges with their ground on the far bank. The construction of Jesus lock and weir raised the water level, to give barges greater depth, and submerged the towpath along the colleges' side. This path had gone under the bridges, but it was not possible to build another higher up that would do the same. Towing of a sort seems to have been done from the bank by means of winches on the barges and ropes attached to posts on the bank. Otherwise the horses towed in the water, as can be seen in prints by Walker and Ackermann. Above Silver Street bridge, which used to be known as the 'Small Bridge', are the *Anchor* and the *Mill*, near the site of King's mill, demolished in 1928. An engraving of 1807 shows two old houses where the *Anchor* now stands and two barges, one loaded with coal and one with grain. The *Anchor* presumably dates from the early nineteenth century when it must have replaced these houses; it is unlikely that either was a pub or the artist would have taken the opportunity to show someone drinking. In 1856 the *Anchor* was revitalised within and was the first pub outside London to incorporate a coffee bar, thus bringing together coffee and alcohol under the same roof after a century or more in which they had been kept generally apart.

The *Mill*, at the foot of Mill Lane, is a sturdy old building, also probably early nineteenth century. It was known until 1890 as the *Hazard Arms*, after Henry Hazard, a coal, corn and timber merchant and maltster who lived in Mill Lane until the 1850s. Another coal and corn merchant, C. F. Foster, who was also a miller, was a neighbour of Hazard's in the lane. He moved his office into the *Ship Inn*, next door to Hazard. As well as business rivals they were also political enemies, Hazard being a keen Tory and Foster an equally keen Liberal. Enmity flared openly when Foster claimed Laundress Lane as his property and put a chain across it, which Hazard kept taking down. Once Foster, who weighed 18 stone, had to hide in his own mill when the angry elderly Hazard pursued him with a horsewhip. The affair led to a court case, decided in Foster's favour in 1853. There was a pub in the same area known as Fosters', and one as Beale's, after another corn merchant. The *Mill* today is a building more in scale with its surroundings than its modern neighbours, but it seems a pity that the brewers have found it necessary to paint their name so garishly on the front and side of the house.

Farther upstream the Newnham mill is remembered by a pub called the *Jolly Miller*, which faces the *Granta* opposite the mill pool. Neither of these houses makes a positive contribution to the appearance of the locality, though the *Granta* supplies excellent sandwiches.

Below the *Pickerel* and Magdalene bridge is Jesus lock. This is the accepted terminus for powered craft, whose crews have three pubs close at hand when mooring below the lock. On the west side is the *Rob Roy*, renamed a few years ago after the local rowing club which once had its headquarters there. It used to be called the *New Spring*, as it stood beside the Spring brewery, and dates from the 1860s. Near Victoria bridge is the *Jolly Waterman*, more riverside in name than in character.

The third pub is the *Fort St George* on Midsummer Common. This used to be even more riverside than it is today; it stood on an island between the course of the river and a lock cut. When the new locks were built in the 1830s this one became redundant and the cut was filled in. There was also a tollhouse on the island and the Fort St George ferry operated from there. The *Fort* dates from the sixteenth century; at one time it probably owned the ferry but this was taken over by the Conservators who built a house next to the pub for the ferryman. It was a chain ferry, carrying warning lights in the days of barge traffic. When the steam barge *Nancy* was operating at the beginning of this century she whistled in advance to give the ferryman warning to slacken his chains to let her pass. Now the ferry has gone, replaced by an ugly but more convenient footbridge. The pub, whose full name used proudly to be the *Fort St George in England*—to distinguish it from the station in India—was extended in the nineteenth century; old pictures often show it flying a particularly large national flag. It joins the *Pickerel* as one of Cambridge's few surviving old inns, and is justifiably popular.

The *Cutter Inn*, from which the Cutter ferry used to run, has been replaced by Banham's boatyard. Farther down, past the gas-works where barges collected gas water, to be used for fertiliser, until 1932, the ferry at the *Green Dragon*, Chesterton, has also been replaced by a footbridge. The *Green Dragon* ran two ferries for many years. It is a very old house, part of a long timber-framed range now comprising three cottages, although the whole range was at one time the pub. A beam cut from a single tree runs the length of the building. The *Green Dragon* was licensed by the Vice-Chancellor of the university in 1630 and had been a victualling house for men and horses for nearly a century before then. It has a fine tiled roof and a sturdy wooden interior, with an early eighteenth-century cupboard and a Victorian painting of itself. It was another popular bargeman's pub and has changed little since the days of riverborne trade.

Equally popular was the *Pike & Eel*, a short walk from the *Green Dragon*, which faces the centre of Stourbridge common across the Cam. Stourbridge is famous as the site of one of Europe's greatest fairs. Here Sir Isaac Newton bought his prisms for £1 each, imported from the continent as English glass was not of sufficient quality. There is a vivid description of the fair, written in 1753:

> The shops or booths are built in rows like streets, each having their name, as Garlick Row, Booksellers' row, Cook-row, etc. And every commodity has its proper place, as the Cheese Fair, Hop Fair, Wool Fair, etc; and here, as in several other streets or rows, are all sorts of traders, who sell by wholesale or retail, as goldsmiths, toy-men, brasiers, turners, milliners, haberdashers, hatters, mercers, drapers, pewterers, china warehouses, and, in a word, most trades that can be found in London, from whence many of them come. Here are also taverns, coffee-houses, and eating-houses in great plenty, and all kept in booths, in any of which (except the coffee-booth) you may at any time be accommo-dated with hot or cold roast goose, roast or boiled pork, etc.

We are told that the heavy goods from London were brought by sea to King's Lynn, and transhipped into barges for Stourbridge. 'More than fifty hackney coaches from London have been

frequently plying at this place, and even wherries, brought from
the Thames in waggons, to row people up and down the Cam.'

Stourbridge Fair ran for three weeks every September, but began
to decline towards the end of the eighteenth century. The *Pike &
Eel* would have seen plenty of activity opposite during the nineteenth century, but the great glory had gone. Now the common is
peaceful except during regattas and the College rowing races; it is
rather bleak and featureless, the only reminder of the fair being
the name of Garlic Row nearby. At the *Pike & Eel* the towpath
begins; it was outside the pub that the horses used to be urged into
the water to haul the remaining part of the journey up to Cambridge. It is a pleasant building—two buildings rather, two small
cottages knocked together. It is one of the rowing landmarks, like
the *Plough* at Fen Ditton about a mile downstream. This was
another ferry crossing. The *Plough* has been a favourite pub with
generations of Cambridge undergraduates. On its lawns crowds
gather to watch the bumps in spring and summer and diners are
summoned from the river bank by tannoy to collect their food
from the bar. Its popularity has not led to drastic modernisation
of its interior, which retains many features of Victorian character.

The *Bridge Hotel* at Clayhithe has a long history. From a point
near here the Romans cut the Caer Dyke, which linked the Cam
to the Witham near Lincoln. Part of the course of this waterway,
which was probably navigable although definitive proof is lacking, can be seen alongside the airfield at Waterbeach on A11, the
Cambridge–Ely road. As the dyke has been disused for something
like 1,800 years, the *Slap Up Inn* on A11 cannot be said to qualify
as a waterside pub. A ferry across the Cam at Clayhithe, however,
is recorded in 1279 when the land at the crossing was in the
possession of Denny Abbey, and the *Bridge* may stand on the site
of a hostel belonging to the abbey. The present building is partly
eighteenth century; an undergraduate's diary records a visit there
in 1795. By 1856 it belonged to Lady Beresford, who sold it in
that year together with a farm, a tollhouse and a brick factory, all
part of the same property. It was known then as the *Pike & Eel*.
Bullard's Brewery bought it in 1895, paying £1,748; soon after it
was renamed (perhaps unofficially) the *House of Lords*, and then in
1912 it became the *Bridge Inn*. Mr Frank Rice, the tenant, ran a

small zoo at the inn, a visit to which was a popular boat outing from Cambridge. Sadly, in 1916 the zoo was closed; the bear was slaughtered and roasted on a spit and sold in sandwiches to raise money for comforts for the troops. The Revd C. F. Farrar called there for a meal while on his voyage described in *Ouse's Silent Tide*, first published in 1921. Having had his request for lunch at another pub regarded as 'an unreasonable and indelicate suggestion' he was delighted to find this 'charming riverside hostel . . . quite a gay place', with houseboats moored nearby, motorboats flitting up and down, and a 2ft watermark on the wallpaper showing the height of a recent flood. He enjoyed an excellent lunch, and the *Bridge*, a free house for many years, preserves the tradition. There is a riverside lawn, the Cam Conservancy yard opposite, and the inevitable caravans are neatly tucked away nearly out of sight.

The riverside pub probably most beloved by the sporting members of Cambridge University was the *Lord Nelson* at Upware—better known as the *Five Miles from Anywhere—No Hurry*. Here in 1851 the Upware Republic was founded by a group of undergraduates devoted to shooting, fishing, the study of nature and the drinking of beer. The Republic lasted for about 15 years, to be succeeded after a decade by a kingdom ruled by a graduate of Jesus College, Richard Ramsay Fielder, who fought the bargemen, drank enormously, spouted ideas and wrote atrocious verse. Calling himself 'His Majesty' he lived at the inn for several years, a richly full-blooded character who made his own contribution to the local gaiety of life. The '*No Hurry*' survived his abdication but was unfortunately burnt down before the war and has not been replaced. Below Clayhithe the river is publess, until the *Fish & Duck* at Pope's Corner, where Cam meets Ouse. This was a little watermen's pub for many years but closed through lack of trade when barge traffic diminished. It became used as a cowhouse, but with the recent increase in pleasure cruising has been entirely rebuilt as a bright and glossy establishment surprising to find in this corner of the Fens.

From Pope's Corner upstream the Ouse is known as the Old West River, a placid, undemanding waterway where the chief visual attraction is usually the wide and swiftly changing sky. Stretham Old Engine is 1½ miles along; built in 1831 it retains its

steam-powered machinery and scoop wheel 37ft in diameter
which lifted as much as 120 tons of water an hour from Waterbeach Fen into the river. There is no ferry at Stretham Ferry,
where a bridge takes the main road over the river beside the *Royal
Oak*, which has ample space for mooring behind it. Next comes
the *Bridge* at Twentypence. This house changed hands in 1973 and
has been brought up to date. Basically it is a simple brick house
facing the river, probably dating from the early nineteenth century. For many years it had remained unaltered—some might say
comfortless. The beer was drawn straight from the barrels and in
winters draught beer was not available as the trade did not merit
it. Until very recently it can hardly have been regarded as a
valuable property; the brewery which bought it about 1950 paid
only £600 for the house and 5 acres of land, and the licensee was a
farmer as well as an innkeeper—a reversion to an old way of life
uncommonly met with in the twentieth century. So little was it
regarded, in fact, that the bar had been painted only twice in 23
years. With a new restaurant, it is now called the *Twentypence Inn*.

From Twentypence the narrow river wanders westward to
Hermitage lock and the entrance in succession to the New and
Old Bedford rivers. The New Bedford brings the tidal water up
from Denver and its effect is noticeable on this next stretch. The
Ouse is much busier here with pleasure craft in the summer
months, though the pubs do not come too frequently. At Earith
the *Crown* provides moorings but turns its face to the road. At
Overcote, above the next lock, Brownshill, is another *Pike & Eel*.
This bears the date 1604 on a lintel and it is likely that half of the
building has been a pub since then. The other half, now incorporated in the inn, was the ferry house for Overcote ferry, which
operated until the floods of 1947; shortly after then it was sunk in
a University Rag celebration. Before Vermuyden's massive
drainage operations there was a ford at Overcote; one effect of the
scheme was to increase the depth of the river here and the line of
the ford is now 5ft under water. The *Pike & Eel* was extended
after the war but has kept an appearance in harmony with the
riverside setting.

Around a bend in the river is Holywell, with the *Ferry Boat Inn*
about which many legends have accumulated. It is one of the

many claimants to the title of Britain's oldest inn, the date you select for its foundation depending upon your degree of credulity. The earliest you can choose is AD 560, but, not surprisingly, evidence is lacking. The church nearby is mentioned in the Domesday Book and can be traced back to 980, but the oldest part of the present building is thirteenth century. Holywell gets its name from a spring in the churchyard. Some local opinion has it that an inn on this site preceded the church and has been there since 890; another date given for its origin is 1068. This last suggestion ties in with the Holywell ghost, the Lady in White, Juliet Tewsley, who hanged herself from a tree after being rejected by her lover Thomas Zoul, a woodcutter from the village. As a suicide she was buried at the crossroads instead of in consecrated ground, and a large flagstone was placed over her grave. We are even told the date, 17 March 1050. Then some years later someone ignorant of this story arrived to build a pub, saw this large flagstone and built his pub around it. Hence the *Ferry Boat Inn*, built in the middle of a crossroads one arm of which disappeared into the river a few yards away. And every 17 March, cunningly disregarding the alterations to the calendar made by that interfering Pope Gregory, Juliet arises from her tomb, points to the flagstone and disappears in the direction of the river. It's a nice story, and a lot of beer has been sold on the strength of it.

The *Ferry Boat* is thatched and half-timbered. Half-timbered is not strictly accurate for the entire building; underneath the applied wood are old brick walls, but it still looks pretty. There is some old timbering inside and the floor has been there for a long time, but it has been worn down by bargemen's boots rather than medieval slippers. For years it was a bargees' pub; they slept in the bar overnight and there was some stabling for their horses at the rear. Corn and grain were the main cargoes, corn being ground at Swanning mill, 3 miles up Cobolds Drain opposite Holywell. More real than Juliet Tewsley is the memory of Mr Arnold, great-grandfather of the present water-bailiff. This gentleman, 5ft 6in tall and weighing 19 stone, used to keep order in the bar. His approach was simple; he offered quarrelling bargees the choice of continuing to fight or accepting a quart of beer. As he was able to lift up one man in each hand and knock their heads

together, they learnt to choose the beer. The door between the
two halves of the bar, which compelled Mr Arnold to turn side-
ways if he wished to get through, has since been removed. The
pub was also used by ferry passengers until the old chain ferry, a
central pontoon with two lifting aprons, was washed away in
1940. The *Ferry Boat* at Holywell is, without overstatement, an
interesting pub.

St Ives has a famous bridge with a chapel, one of only four such
remaining in the country; there are plenty of inns in the town but
none strictly riverside. There is indeed a dearth of riverside pubs
on the upper reaches of the Ouse. There used to be several, but
with the decline of commercial traffic on the upper river in the
mid-nineteenth century many of them closed. At Huntingdon the
rambling *Old Bridge Hotel*, a coaching inn, edges towards the
river. It is a conglomeration of buildings, some parts eighteenth
century, and includes the offices of an eighteenth-century bank,
Rust's Bank, whose vaults are somewhere underneath the bar.
There is another *Bridge Hotel* at St Neots, near the site of the
medieval priory, a carved stone from which is set in the outside
wall. Parts of this building are very old, the site being presumably
that of a hostel for the priory by the bridge first built in 1180.
Both these hotels have very good restaurants.

Navigation on the upper Ouse continues as far as Great Barford
lock, a few miles from Bedford, with two *Anchors*, one at Temps-
ford, the other at Great Barford, on the way. The River Authority
are reopening the navigation to Bedford, with three more locks
to be reconstructed. About 4 miles of river in the area administered by Bedford Corporation are navigable now, with some
splendid establishments along the banks. When the link is completed, there will be a navigable river from Bedford to the Wash—
a distance of nearly 85 miles via the Old West.

Back now to Pope's Corner, and downstream towards Denver
Sluice and King's Lynn. The course of the river by Ely is artificial,
probably cut in the early days of the religious settlement at Ely,
bringing the facility for water transport nearer to the foot of the
hill on which the abbey stood and from which now the great
cathedral dominates the Fens. It formed part of a 'stone route',
by which building stone from Barnack was conveyed to Ely and

to Peterborough as well. For several centuries the river was Ely's main artery of transport, what few roads there were being often unusable except in summer. Ely was a boat-building centre with a quay, several wharves or hithes and many warehouses and granaries. Naturally there was also a large number of pubs; the *Anchor*, the *Ship*, the *Seven Stars*, the *Jolly Waterman* and more. Today there is only one, the *Cutter*.

The *Cutter* stands on the site of a brewery and maltings; the lane leading to the rear of the pub used to be called Beer Lane in the seventeenth century. But there was no actual pub until the completion of the New Cut on the river in 1830. This cut was a straight channel from a point about half a mile north of Ely to Littleport, avoiding a dog-leg voyage through Prickwillow and a bed of troublesome shallows known as the Ely hards. The improvement to navigation brought increased trade to Ely, and Morley Wright Cutlack, who owned the maltings on the site next to the quay at Annesdale, obtained a licence to retail beer. So Mr Cutlack opened his pub because of the New Cut, and called it the *Cutter*. The present sign, pretty though it may be, is not very relevant. More appropriate would be a brawny character with a shovel, as 'cutter' is a regional equivalent of 'navvy'. For the first few years the inn does not seem to have been very prosperous. It was sold and the licence was not renewed; then in 1841 it was put up for auction. The property included 'a commodious brick Dwelling-house with Counting-house and other necessary offices; Yard, Garden, Stables and Coach House. An extensive Malting . . . a Malting kiln, Malt Chamber and Granaries. A small but convenient Brewery. The *Cutter Inn* adjoining'. For a time no one would buy it, but by 1844 it was back in action, some of the buildings being used to store coal and other heavy freight and the coach-house being converted into a skittle alley. From now on the *Cutter* appears in countless pictorial views of Ely Cathedral, crouched in the right foreground with a boat or two beside it and the cathedral looming above. Looking with keen eyes at these pictures one can trace the changes in the breweries providing its beers.

The *Cutter* was modernised in 1964 and the various buildings that used to be attached to it were swept away for a car park.

Maltings do survive on the waterfront, but used for a different purpose. Harlock's maltings, built in 1868, were sold after a fire in 1967 by their then owners, Watneys, to Ely UDC for a nominal sum for conversion into a public hall. Both the Ely Maltings and the *Cutter* became more widely known to boating people from all over the country when the National Rally of Boats was held in Ely in 1973. Nearly 300 boats, probably more at one time than had ever been gathered together in Ely before during all its riverine history, congregated along the river banks, and *Albion*, the last trading wherry under sail, turned a new page in waterway history when she sailed up the Ouse at the end of her voyage from Yarmouth to moor outside the *Cutter*, the first (and last) Norfolk wherry to sail in the Fenland waters.

The diversion of the Ouse through the New Cut left a riverside pub, the *Plough*, isolated. The *Plough*, whose structure contained stone destined for ecclesiastical building at Ely and thrown overboard to lighten vessels to enable them to float over the Ely hards, stood just to the north of a point where the original course of the Lark met the original course of the Ouse, according to A. K. Astbury, an expert on this subject, who recounts the changing courses of the Fen rivers in his book *The Black Fens*. It is now a private house, squat, determined-looking, with a massive end chimney, a constant in Fenland's changing scene.

The *Black Horse*, on the edge of Littleport, is the survivor of three pubs within a few hundred yards. Two others used to stand on the opposite bank; the older of them called the *Queen Adelaide*. Coal and manure were the two main freights at Littleport. The barge horses knew the pubs at which their masters customarily stopped and would automatically slow down when on the towpath opposite, ready to jump on to the barge to cross the river. Some of these pubs had blackboards with the bargemen's names down one side with room for chalk marks against them to denote the amount of beer consumed. The *Black Horse* is mid-Victorian, opened at a time when pubs on the upper Ouse were closing but trade was still being maintained in the Fens. It possibly remained open because next to it was a standpipe to which villagers from the locality had to come to obtain their drinking water which was filtered through the pipe from the river. The Lark meets the Ouse just above Littleport; on the lower reaches of this river there used to be five pubs some years ago, but there are none today.

The next tributary to join the Ouse is the Little Ouse, or Brandon River. The *Ship Inn* is by the confluence. There was a farmhouse selling beer here in the mid-seventeenth century. It is referred to in deeds dated 1770 as the *Brandon Creek House*, when it seems to have been a proper inn. The present building dates from about 1840. Until recently it was a plain country inn. It was here that W. H. Barrett heard many of the stories and legends he retold so effectively in *Tales from the Fens*, required reading for anyone wanting to catch the 'feel' of this odd land of quirky characters, hard work and empty skies. This pub, or its immediate predecessor, was the resort of Cadilly, a well-known Cambridge prostitute of the early nineteenth century. She used to pick up undergraduates at the *Little Rose* in Cambridge, where a relation of hers was landlord, and take them out in her boat, called quite naturally the *Willing Maid*, for a week-end frolic at the *Ship*. Mark Twain was another, more reputable, visitor to this pub. The *Ship* had stabling and a forge adjacent; it has been modernised and is now rather smart, with carpets and a dining-room. The riverside setting is very pleasant.

The *Ferry Boat* at Southery, the next pub down, is a great contrast. This is the pub to go to now if you want to recapture the 'Barrett atmosphere'. Here you will hear of Ally Boozer—real name Albert Legge, descendant of the Chafer Legge who told Barrett many of the old Fen tales. Ally's wife Mary has an infallible prescription for the cure of the mange. They will tell you that Ely Cathedral was built by men in boats, constructing it from the top downwards as the water slowly receded. There is no carpet and not much comfort; but you can learn a lot. The old wire ferry, which could take, at some peril, a horse and cart, used to be operated from the bank opposite the pub by an old lady. It stopped working about 1935, but a punt ferry for pedestrians only was in use until recently.

There is only one more pub in the 5 miles from the *Ferry Boat* to Denver; the *Windmill*, by Hilgay bridge. This was rebuilt about 13 years ago; it used to be the toll-keeper's house, the bridge having been a toll bridge until 1929. Half way between the *Wind-*

mill and Denver is the junction with the Wissey, perhaps the most beautiful of the Ouse tributaries and navigable for 7 miles to Stoke Ferry. Then comes Denver Sluice, the key to the drainage of the Fens as it has been called, with the navigation lock on the eastern side and, tucked in between the Ouse and the New Bedford River, the *Jenyns Arms*.

John Jenyns, to whom the pub owes its name, was a member of the Bedford Level Corporation who spoke out strongly against those burgesses of King's Lynn and other towns who maintained in the late seventeenth century that the sluice should be removed as an obstacle to navigation. By diverting the tidal water along the New Bedford, Vermuyden's drainage scheme added great diffi- culties to the problems of water transport between King's Lynn and Cambridge; the absence of tides helped the accumulation of silt and denied assistance to the boats which previously made use of tidal power. Fen drainage is a complicated subject; it may suffice here to say that it has taken about 300 years, with the construc- tion of the Cut-off Channel, to get it, let us hope, more or less right.

The *Jenyns Arms* in the last century provided lodgings for the 'berthsmen', specialist navigators or pilots who worked the boats along the tidal waterway below Denver. They were paid ten shillings a trip. Some also lodged at another public house near the sluice, since gone. At the latter the poker was kept chained to the fireplace, the necessity of which reflects either on the honesty or the peaceableness of the pub's clientele. For crews in action there was a free allowance of beer. At an ordinary halt the skipper claimed a quart, the horse-keeper a pint and the apprentice half a pint; this was trebled for a long stop when cargo was loaded or unloaded. If they wanted any more they had to pay. Generally beer was not carried on the boats, so the pubs did a healthy trade.

Nowadays the *Jenyns Arms* marks the turning point for boats whose crews do not wish—or, in the case of hired boats, are not permitted—to venture into the tidal Ouse. Consequently it is often busy, with sightseers also who drive out to study Denver itself, the A. G. Wright sluice on the Relief Channel and the new sluices on the Cut-off Channel. It provides excellent sandwiches from a bar with an improbable thatched roof. Affixed to the outside of

(*Top*) The *Jenyns Arms*, Denver Sluice; (*Centre*) The *Anchor*, Sutton Gault, on the New Bedford River; (*bottom*) The *Three Tuns*, Welney, on the Old Bedford River

Page 36

(*Above*) The *Trout*, Godstow, about 1875

(*Below*) A room in the *Trout*

the inn is a board with the toll charges that were levied for crossing the sluice until 1963.

On the New Bedford—or Hundred Foot—River there are two pubs. One is the *Three Pickerels*, at Mepal. The present house was built about 1920, replacing the *Three Fishers* which belonged to what was then the river Catchment Board. This was the barge depot for Chatteris, with a granary and storehouses; a row of cottages next to the pub bears the date 1756. In later years, sugar beet and grain were the main cargoes loaded here. The area is now popular with wildfowlers and fishermen; indeed, it has been for centuries. Few boats call here, nor at the second of the New Bedford pubs, the *Anchor* at Sutton Gault. This is a most attractive pub, a low brick house whitewashed in front, facing the water; at the rear there is a fine old barn. The *Anchor* hides behind the river bank, raised after the floods of 1947. Beer comes from barrels; the *Anchor* has been modernised minimally and life therein seems to tick over quietly. There is a painting of the pub in the smoke room; it is not altogether unfair to say that it is one of the few Fenland pubs worth painting at all. On the far side of the twin Bedford rivers is the northern terminal of the ill-fated hovertrain track, never completed from Earith and now abandoned through the withdrawal of government support. A pub called the *Fish and Duck* became part of the Tracked Hovercraft Company's premises, and there was also a *Bell* riverside at the Gault.

To enter the Old Bedford River and make your way along the complex of navigable drains connecting the Ouse system with the Nene it is necessary to pass through the tidal sluice at Salter's Lode, which is opened only for a few minutes each day when the water on either side makes a level. There was a more direct route through Well Creek until it became impassable a few years ago. This is now being restored and as there is a tidal lock at Salter's Lode connecting the Creek with the Ouse the delay while waiting for a level will be much shortened. Well Creek will also give access to a number of pubs in the villages of Upwell and Outwell through which it runs as if it were in Holland. As it is, however, a long run is necessary up the Old Bedford until one turns into the Middle Level at Welches Dam. Along the route there are just two pubs left of the many there once were. There used to be a greater

c

number than would seem to be needed to satisfy the thirsts of
bargemen and farm-workers. This was because they also served
the needs of the many men employed to dig, maintain and repair
the drains and preserve and strengthen the banks against the
possibilities of floods. Some of the pubs were built by the Bedford
Level Corporation and leased by them to tenants. The *Three Tuns*
is the only one left of four waterside pubs at Welney; as it was
near the village its rent was high, at £77 a year, compared to that
of the *Green Man*, an isolated house, which was a mere £5. It is a
plain little brick building, green-washed, near Welney sluice. It
has a friendly atmosphere and is once more getting trade from the
river as more pleasure cruisers percolate into the region.

Under a mile from Welches Dam is the Old Bedford's other
survivor, the *Ship* at Purl's bridge, at the end of a road from
Manea. Purl's footbridge, which had a movable section for the
passage of boats, has gone; so have the licences of four other pubs
between here and Welches Dam. Near the *Ship* were the *Anchor*
and the *Chequers*, and at Welches Dam lock were the *Three Fishes*
and the *Princess Victoria*. Mr William Kent runs the *Ship*, often in
shirtsleeves and wellington boots; his grandmother used to run
it, and he was born in the pub next door. The *Ship* has no bar, no
slot machines, no indoor games; the beer is good, coming, as at
the Sutton Gault *Anchor*, direct from the barrel. This is a fine
place for the ornithologist studying the bird life of the Ouse
Washes. It is also a fine place for reminiscences of the days of
Jackson's Navy—the gangs of lighters run by Vic Jackson of
Stanground in the years between the wars. Mr Kent remembers
watching Vic Jackson bring a gang of eight lighters around the
right-angled bend out of Welches Dam lock into the Old Bedford
without uncoupling them—and without, as he ought to have
done, penning them through the lock one by one. Time being
money, Vic would never waste it. The lighters referred to were
the craft especially developed for the Fen waterways, flat-bot-
tomed, between 40 and 50ft long, able to load about 25 tons and
drawing 3½ft. They worked in 'gangs', fastened each to each and
towed by horses and later by steam tugs. One lighter in each
gang had a cabin; this was known as the 'house lighter'. There
were also horse boats, used for ferrying horses across the river

when the towpath changed sides, and the small 'Fen boats' employed on the narrow loads and drains.

The lock at Welches Dam leads into the Forty Foot but because of the dimensions of the locks no craft more than 46ft long can use the Middle Level. There was a *Three Fishers* by the Forty Foot, photographed by Sir Benjamin Stone in 1905, but this, like any other pubs there were along the way, has gone. There are, however, pubs enough in March and Whittlesey. One of the March pubs, a nice old house called the *Ship*, faces the Old Nene—which connects with the Forty Foot via the Sixteen Foot and Popham's Eau. Certainly it is complicated, made more so by the fact that now the Sixteen Foot is wider than the Forty Foot and no one pronounces Eau in the same way as anyone else does. Apart from the *Ship Inn*, March has the hardy Middle Level Watermen's Club near to the thatched *White Horse* and, according to Lord Orford who undertook a pleasure cruise on these waters in 1784 with a fleet of four boats, a horse boat, three tenders and a bum-ketch all drawn by a horse called Hippopotamus, it was the handsomest town he had yet seen. He and his company were surprised by what he described as 'the disagreeable arrangement of features called ugliness' of the women. On enquiry, however, his surprise ceased, 'when we were informed that this part of the country was settled by a colony of Dutch about the time of the Revolution, which accounted for the squat shape, flat nose, round unmeaning face which prevails amongst the inhabitants'. In this respect at least, one hastens to add, the outlook has changed.

Orford gives graphic descriptions of sailing and fishing on Whittlesey Mere, once the largest lake in the southern half of England, 3,000 acres in winter, drained in 1850 and now rich arable land. Whittlesey itself has several pubs, including the *Boat* by the waterside and the *Hero of Aliwal*, once very popular with lightermen, a few yards away. The hero was Sir Harry Smith, born in the town, who was a well-known soldier and led the charge against the Sikhs at Aliwal in 1846. There is also a pub called the *Letter B*, but no one seems to know why. In her book *Fenland Chronicle* Sybil Marshall recalls her father's descriptions of the Fenland pubs. He was for some time a waterman—he says how he was sometimes pushed into the river by his horse jumping

aboard for a rest when the boats got close in to the bank—and he
enjoyed the company in the pubs as well as the drink. Some of the
landlords kept nuts and dates; a group would call for a pint of
'Barceloneys', empty them in a heap on the table and draw one
nut in turn. The one left with the last nut had to pay for the lot.
His wife remembered the floating church, constructed on a barge
that travelled the waterways while the church at Holme was being
rebuilt; she knew several people who were christened on board.

The Middle Level connects with the Nene through the lock at
Stanground. Downriver is the port of Wisbech and the outfall
into the Wash; this is the route for craft too long for the Middle
Level. The river here runs in a straight artificial cut, the waters
controlled by the Dog-in-a-Doublet sluice just under 6 miles
below Peterborough. The area takes its name from the pub a few
hundred yards below the sluice. There are only a few pubs sharing
this name, which was once referred to by Dr Johnson to illustrate
a point. Talking about an old idea expressed in a new way, he
said: 'It is an old coat with new facing.' Then, laughing heartily,
'it is the old dog in a new doublet.' This particular *Dog* dates from
the middle of the seventeenth century and seems always to have
been a licensed house. River Board meetings began to be held
here in 1752. The River Board owned the house for years; in its
history it housed the lock-keeper toll-collector, as well as selling
beer. It was a well-known haunt of wildfowlers. About 1845 it
was described as a 'rude hostel' with an 'antediluvian ostler' by
Horace William Wheelwright, in his *Sporting Sketches at Home and
Abroad*. There he met 'the king of the Fen gunners' and on
another occasion a group of 'navvies', workers on the maintenance of the navigation who lodged there from time to time. The
Dog was originally a three-storey building; it still is at the rear,
but lost its front ground floor when the river bank was raised.
Some extensions have been added recently and it is no longer
'rude' in any sense. But as you stand with your back to the house,
with the sluggish river flowing in front of you, the gaunt structure of the sluice away to your right and to your left the bridge
and then space, flatness, stillness . . . it is lonely, eerie even. Here
there are times when one can welcome the sight and sound of a
passing car.

Peterborough now has nearly 2 miles of fine moorings, a theatre within a few yards of the river, an old Custom House—but no waterside pub. Indeed the Nene is a comparatively publess river altogether. There are pubs in the villages, but the Nene avoids the villages—or rather the other way about, for this river was for centuries notorious for flooding and most of the settlements were built at a safe distance, as a glance at the map makes clear. Nor was the Nene ever a really successful through navigation for commercial traffic; in fact it is likely that it is busier today with pleasure cruisers than it ever was with commercial craft. Peterborough might yet become an inland port, but upstream there are too many low bridges and the river too often takes the longest distance between two points for there to be any hope of restoration of trading using the river's natural course.

The village of Wansford did become a river port for about 100 years after the navigation was improved in the mid-eighteenth century, and there are still some reminders to be found including the wharf house, granaries and the Nene Barge & Lighter Co, still in existence. The Great North Road crossed the river at Wansford bridge; fortunately it by-passes the village today or there might not be much village left. It was the road that was the reason for the Nene's most famous inn, the *Haycock*, which was a posting house beside the bridge, built on the site of an earlier inn in 1632. The present front entrance used to be an arch through which the coaches passed for passengers to alight in the courtyard, while the horses were tethered in the archway to the inner yard. The *Haycock*, one of the largest inns built in the seventeenth century, provided stabling for 150 horses, a loft for cockfighting and its own brewhouse. It is famous for the adventure of 'drunken Barnaby', described in modest verse by Richard Braithwaite, in 1638:

> On a haycock sleeping soundly
> The river rose and took me roundly
> Down the current: people cried,
> As along the stream I hied.
> 'Where away?' quoth they. 'From Greenland?'
> 'No: from Wansford Bridge in England.'

The incident provided the inn with its name in later years, when it was changed from the *Swan* to the *Haycock*. The sign recalls the incident; a much earlier sign, bearing the vestiges of a picture similar to that on the present one, is preserved behind glass above the 'cooling arch' in the courtyard. The flooding that caused Barnaby's adventure may have been deliberately brought about by the drawing of flashes to float barges loaded with slate down the river, possibly even to the *Haycock* itself which is roofed with what was said to be over an acre of Collyweston slate. Deliberate flooding was not unknown on the Nene in more recent years when barges were delayed by insufficient depth of water; the admiral of Jackson's Navy, referred to above, could bear witness on this matter.

The *Haycock* was praised by that indefatigable and critical traveller Viscount Torrington, who commented in his diary in 1790: 'This is a nice Inn. Everything clean and in good order, the beds and stabling excellent.' He also described it as 'the best of Inns, pleasantly situated; the bridge, the river, the church beyond, and all about contributes to the right Inn scenery'. It maintained its reputation well into the next century, being considered of suitable standard to accommodate the Duchess of Kent and her daughter Princess Victoria Alexandrina on their journey north to visit the Archbishop of York in 1835, two years before the young princess was crowned queen. She gave her portrait to the inn in recognition of the hospitality received. It became well-known as a sporting centre; the great Fred Archer began his career as a jockey from the *Haycock*, and the hunting centred on Wansford drew many wealthy visitors from abroad. Business, however, declined as the century drew on until Mrs Percival, who owned it at the time, decided in 1887 to give up the trade and turned the place into a farm, relinquishing the licence a few years later. It passed through many hands in the following years, for some time being a racing stable with over a hundred horses, run by Lionel Digby. In 1914 it was bought by Sir Bache Cunard, of the shipping family, a famous sportsman. Soon after the war began he installed his own ordnance factory in the premises, producing shell bases and other armaments accessories. It was Sir Bache who effected in the garden the topiarist representation of Barnaby on his haycock, which, unfortunately, has had to be cut right back—let us hope it will grow again. He died in 1925 and his collection of splendid eighteenth-century furniture was auctioned at the house. Then Lord Fitzwilliam took the place over, and in 1928 he got the licence restored even though he had to appeal eventually to the House of Lords to win his case. The *Haycock* is now in the same management as the *Old Bridge* at Huntingdon. It is a lovely old building, full of character and interest, the walls lined with good sporting prints. Even the floor of the ballroom, in what used to be the laundry, has historical connections; it once formed part of the stage of the Royal Opera House, Covent Garden, and has borne the weight of many famous feet. One intriguing question, however, is left unanswered: what were the 'Shady Adventures' which Mr Swann, MP, enjoyed at the *Haycock* in 1802 that led to his being accused in the House of Commons of bribery and corruption?

There is plenty of history along this stretch of the Nene. Below Wansford is Castor, a major Roman settlement and pottery centre; above is Fotheringhay where Edmund Langley, a son of Edward III and founder of the House of York, founded a college with an imposing collegiate church. Today of this foundation only the nave and west tower of the church remain. Within the church are the tombs of Edward, Duke of York, killed at Agincourt, and of his nephew Richard Plantagenet and his wife, Cicely, mother of Edward IV and Richard III. There was a castle at Fotheringhay, built in the eleventh century. Richard III was born here. Under the Tudors it became a state prison, and here Mary Queen of Scots was tried in 1586 and executed in February of the following year. The historian J. A. Froude describes the formal preparations, the dignity of the Queen, smiling and composed. She bade her ladies adieu, prayed, and, her eyes bound with a handkerchief, lowered her head on to the block. At first the headsman was nervous and the axe missed its mark; but at the second blow the severed head fell; 'and at once a metamorphosis was witnessed, strange as ever was wrought by wand of fabled enchanter. The coif fell off and the false plaits. The laboured illusion vanished. The lady who had knelt before the block was in the maturity of grace and loveliness. The executioner, when he raised the head as usual to show it to the crowd, exposed the withered features of a grizzled, wrinkled old woman . . .' The castle, of which the Nene formed part of the outer moat, was demolished by the Stuarts; there is only a grassy mound, crowned with nettles, to show where it stood. Amongst the nettles the devoted still leave tributes to the Plantagenets and to the Scottish queen.

The villages near the Nene—Nassington, Fotheringhay, Tansor —with their cottages built of the local stone and their manor houses of some grandeur are unspoiled and beautiful. But they keep the river at a remove, and there are no waterside inns. Yet much of the stone for these villages came by the river. The small town of Oundle, built inside a loop of the Nene, has whole streets of stone buildings, harmonious and carefully preserved. When the castle at Fotheringhay was demolished, some of the stones were used in the rebuilding of the *Talbot Hotel* in New Street, in 1626. A pub on the north-east of Oundle is actually called the *Riverside Inn*, but it is something of a misnomer, being separated from the river by the derelict railway. The only pub on the Middle Nene that can really be called riverside is probably the *King's Head* at Wadenhoe, a few miles above Oundle. This is riverside by virtue of the moorings at the foot of its garden; it is an old village pub, part-thatched, part-slate roof. The *Cottage Inn* near Welling-borough and the little *Railway Inn* at Irthlingborough are not too far away, but after a long haul the *Britannia* on the approach to Northampton comes as some relief. Here it is easy for boat crews to tie up and refresh themselves after—or before—the succession of guillotine lock gates, to wind each of which takes about 130 turns of the windlass. There is one more lock before Northampton and the Town lock leading to the entrance to the Northampton arm of the Grand Union and thence, as Priestley would say, 'to all parts of the kingdom'. Northampton itself, the scene of Water Festivals and a successful National Rally of Boats, has become river-conscious; the river now is an amenity and not, as in previous centuries, a threat to life and health.

3

RIVERSIDE 2
The Thames

The number of Thames-side pubs is enormous. In his book devoted to those on the tidal river between Teddington and Shoeburyness, Glyn Morgan lists 131, although some of these are not strictly riverside. The number of surviving pubs originally built or licensed to serve the riverborne traffic is far less, but it is sometimes difficult to make precise distinctions. Except for the local historian the matter is of little significance now; the character of the river has changed so much, and the character of the frequenters of the pubs likewise, that what links there are between past and present may be more apparent than real. By no means does this imply that everything is fake. But, with a natural desire to attract the tourist trade, brewers and landlords have clearly set out in certain instances to anticipate the tastes of their clientele, and it is not always easy to sympathise with what Dr Johnson called 'the wild vicissitudes of taste'.

A really full-blooded effort to recreate the past is shown in one of the newest London pubs, called *Samuel Pepys at Brooks Wharf.*

This is a conversion of part of a warehouse near Southwark bridge and is designed to show various aspects of the life of Samuel Pepys. The downstairs bar is intended to remind you of a riverside warehouse in the days of Charles II, and five of the tables in the restaurant upstairs are set in a facsimile four-poster bed. A daily quotation from Pepys' *Diary* is found next to the teleprinter. As Pepys himself said, 'it is pretty to see what money will do'. It is pretty also in the *Mayflower* at Rotherhithe which after war damage was rebuilt inside to simulate a seventeenth-century inn of the type those well-known roisterers, the Pilgrim Fathers, would doubtless have been acquainted with. The fabric of the *Mayflower* is eighteenth century, but previously the site had been occupied by an inn, the *Ship*, since 1550. Its interior decor apart, the *Mayflower* has two outstanding features—a balcony overlooking the river, and the right to sell British and American postage stamps, never rescinded since it was first granted for the convenience of seamen.

The oldest London riverside pub seems to be the famous *Prospect of Whitby*, at Wapping Wall. This dates from 1520; it was renamed, having previously been called the *Devil's Tavern*, in 1777, after a Whitby sailing vessel called *The Prospect* which used to moor nearby. It is firmly embedded in the tourist circuit, not surprisingly in view of its situation and literary and artistic associations. The *Town of Ramsgate*, near the *Prospect*, makes an interesting contrast. A small and comfortable pub, originally called the *Red Cow*, it retains the little bar rooms which so many establishments have done away with, perhaps on the advice of an interior decorator, perhaps so that no one may drink unobserved by keen-eyed landlord or bartender.

Among other well-known London pubs is the *Angel*, near the *Mayflower* at Rotherhithe, with a view of the Pool of London and Tower Bridge, updated to cope with more fashionable customers than it used to entertain. In Southwark the eighteenth-century *Anchor*, in a part of London rich in associations with Shakespeare and Dr Johnson, has been extended and contains an interesting collection of historical relics and reminders. Near the entrance lock to the Regent's Canal, the *Grapes*—the original of Dickens' *Six Jolly Fellowship Porters*—has changed little in appearance over the years. 'It was a narrow lopsided wooden jumble of corpulent windows heaped one upon another as you might heap as many toppling oranges, with a crazy wooden veranda impending over the water; indeed the whole house, inclusive of the complaining flag-staff on the roof, impended over the water, but seemed to have got into the condition of a faint-hearted diver who has paused so long on the brink that he will never go in at all.' So Dickens describes the house in *Our Mutual Friend*, a book which is a useful corrective to an over-romantic view of London's riverside 150 years ago, 'where accumulated scum of humanity seemed to have been washed from higher grounds like so much moral sewage, and to be pausing until its own weight forced it over the bank and sunk it in the river'. Under the rule of Miss Potterson, the *Six Jolly Fellowship Porters* was an island of respectability in this area.

Another Dickens pub is the *Trafalgar*, famous in the past for whitebait suppers, reopened fairly recently after being shut for nearly 60 years. This is one of a trio of Greenwich pubs, the others being the *Yacht* and the *Cutty Sark*. The *Yacht* has been in continuous occupation for the longest time; the other two date from earlier years of the nineteenth century, although the *Cutty Sark*, renamed after the clipper found a permanent home nearby, succeeded previous inns on the same site dating back to Tudor times. There is a feel of Dickens too at the *Lobster Smack* on Canvey Island, in the country of *Great Expectations*. Over 400 years old, the *Lobster Smack* redeems its environs from total architectural disaster—a long, low weather-boarded building which might not look so exceptional elsewhere but here provides welcome aesthetic satisfaction.

Upriver, far from the marshes and the memories of smugglers and the hulks—the old convict ships—and away from the diminishing glories of London's dockland, are equally famous pubs. The *Doves* at Hammersmith, once a coffee house, is one of them. Two vessels are recalled at Strand-on-the-Green: the *Steam Packet* and the *City Barge*. The latter dates from the end of the fifteenth century, but its name comes from the *Maria Wood*, the barge belonging to the Corporation of London, launched in 1816, which was moored in this reach of the river. At Isleworth the

three-storey Georgian *London Apprentice*, possibly so named because apprentices from London used to row here for a drink—or
possibly after the London Apprentice who married the daughter of
the King of Turkey, as described in an old but improbable ballad—
has been a popular resort since it was built, and before then as
an inn had been on this site for 300 years before the present one.

There is some risk of generalisation, but on the whole the
London riverside pubs do little trade with customers coming
directly off the river. In many of them the entrace of a waterman
or lighterman would cause great consternation, though some in
the City and East End might take what comes with equanimity,
and there are a few licensed to open especially early for dock-
workers. On the glossier reaches of the non-tidal Thames many
of the pubs would reject this appellation with contempt; whatever they once were, they are now hotels. Some of them are rightly
famous for their cooking or the resources of their wine cellars.
Splendid cruisers can be found at their moorings, the inland
waterway equivalents of the Jaguars and Rovers to be seen in the
car parks. There are, of course, plenty of reminders of the river's
history. The *Donkey House Hotel* at Windsor was once a popular
call for crews of Thames barges; the *Compleat Angler* at Marlow
recalls a certain book about fishing. There are two beautifully
situated houses at Sonning, the *French Horn* and the *White Hart*,
the latter dating from the fourteenth century. Another old one is
the deplorably spelt *Ye Olde Leatherne Bottel* at Goring, also
popular with bargemen for centuries.

The *Beetle and Wedge* at Moulsford, by a public landing place
where there used to be a ferry on the route of the old Ridgeway, is
a classic Thames-side pub. Many decades ago it had a well-known
fictional visitor, who 'stopped at the sight of the place and surveyed its deep tiled roof, nestling under big trees . . . its sign
towards the roadway, its sun-blistered green bench and tables, its
shapely white windows and its row of upshooting hollyhock
plants in the garden. . . . The windows on the ground floor were
long and low, and they had pleasing red blinds. The green tables
outside were agreeably ringed with memories of former drinks,
and an extensive grape vine spread level branches across the whole
front of the place. Against the wall was a broken oar, two boat-

hooks, and the stained and faded red cushions of a pleasure boat. One went up three steps to the glass-panelled door and peeped into a broad, low room with a bar and beer-engine, behind which were many bright and helpful-looking bottles against mirrors, and great and little pewter measures, and bottles fastened in brass wire upside down, with their corks replaced by taps, and a white china cask labelled 'Shrub', and cigar boxes, and boxes of cigarettes, and a couple of Toby jugs and a beautifully coloured hunting scene framed and glazed, showing the most elegant people taking Piper's Cherry Brandy . . .' The visitor was Mr Polly, and the *Beetle and Wedge* was the original of the *Potwell Inn*, where took place the defeat of Uncle Jim and where Mr Polly settled into a new and satisfying way of life. Although larger than one imagined it, the pub is still recognisable from Wells' description. The house takes its name from the tools used in log-splitting, logs at one time being floated down the river to London from here. The present building is early nineteenth century, but it stands on a very old inn site.

At Streatley there is an old *Swan*, and at Sandford lock the *King's Arms*, the only lockside pub on the river. Above Oxford at Binsey the *Perch* has gardens leading down to the river; this is an interesting sixteenth-century house, perhaps less interesting in that it has lost its small drinking rooms in favour of one large bar. Then in another mile is one of the most distinguished Thames-side inns, the *Trout*, overlooking the weir at Godstow.

The present building mainly dates from 1646 and has changed little since then. Its predecessor was a hospice attached to Godstow nunnery, a Benedictine foundation of Dame Ediva of Winchester about 1138. Rosamund Clifford, mistress of Henry II, for whom the king constructed a secret bower by his hunting lodge at Woodstock to keep his meetings with her hidden from the suspicious eyes of Queen Eleanor, died in this nunnery in 1176. She was being educated in the nunnery when the king first saw her; she bore him two children, and legend ascribes her death to poisoning at the hands of the jealous queen. But there is no evidence of Eleanor's responsibility. After her death Rosamund (Rosa Mundi—Rose of the World) took on the status of a local heroine; the liberally—and perhaps politically—minded nuns buried her in a superb tomb and worshipped her memory. After the dissolution of the monasteries the nunnery became a private house, and was destroyed after being besieged by Sir Thomas Fairfax in 1646. Stones from the ruins were used to enlarge the hospice, which became an inn. The remains of the nunnery are on the far side of the river from the Trout.

Fred Thacker, historian of the Thames, described the *Trout* as 'a pleasant house, with its shady alleys, waterside bowers and rustic bridge'. The bridge is at least a century old, though now it is used only by the peacocks when, surfeited with sandwiches, they go to inspect the collection of stone ornaments in the elaborate garden. With its terrace alongside the weir stream the *Trout* for decades—centuries—has been extremely popular. The single storey extensions, built recently to cope with the demand, fortunately harmonise well enough with the old stone frontage. Apart from these extensions, and a mild rash of bungalows nearby, the river hereabout cannot have changed much since 4 July 1862 when the Mathematical Lecturer of Christ Church, Oxford, took the three small daughters of the Dean for a trip up the river to Godstow; 'we had tea on the bank there,' he noted in his diary, 'and did not reach Christ Church until half-past eight'. Three years later, the Revd Charles Dodgson published the story he began to tell the girls on that sunny afternoon. *Alice's Adventures in Wonderland* was the name of the book; the author called himself Lewis Carroll.

There are two other *Trouts* on the Thames above Oxford, but they are some distance away and the upper river is no waterway to hurry along. At Bablock Hythe, nearer to Oxford by road than river, Matthew Arnold saw the Scholar Gipsy:

> For most, I know, thou lov'st retired ground.
>   Thee, at the ferry, Oxford riders blithe,
>   Returning home on summer nights have met
>   Crossing the stripling Thames at Bablock-hithe,
>   Trailing in the cool stream thy fingers wet,
>   As the slow punt swings round:
>   And leaning backwards in a pensive dream,
>   And fostering in thy lap a heap of flowers
>   Pluck'd in shy fields and distant Wychwood bowers,
>   And thine eyes resting on the moonlit stream . . .

Or at least he imagined he saw him, because the story of the scholar who left the university to join a gipsy tribe was two hundred years old when Arnold wrote his poem. If excuse is needed for quoting from it, it is that there is nothing one can say so evocatively about Bablock Hythe today. The ferry operates no more; the fields sprout caravans obtrusively. By the old ferry crossing the *Ferry* provides every facility for boaters, caravanners and chalet dwellers; but, to make no more of it, it is not what it was when it used to be the *Chequers*.

At Newbridge, where the Windrush joins the Thames and A415 crosses it, there is a pub on each side of the river, one in Oxfordshire and one in Berkshire. The New Bridge was originally built about 1250; it was new when compared to the bridge at Radcot. The Oxfordshire pub is the *Rose Revived*, which may have started life as a hermitage giving the revenue it obtained from visitors towards the upkeep of the bridge. At some stage in its history it became an alehouse called the *Chequers*, belonging to Lincoln College, for which the tenant paid an annual rental of 3s 4d. Later it became the *Rose*, and later still was rebuilt and extended as the *Rose Revived*. It is a fine Cotswold building, a hotel and restaurant of some quality and style with lawns down to the river. The *Rose Revived*, like a few others of the upper Thames inns, is a model of how to introduce modern comfort and amenity into an old building without destroying the atmosphere or debauching the surrounding area.

It is no longer necessary for enthusiastic drinkers to run from the *Maybush* to the *Rose Revived* for the extra half hour when the former pub closed at the early Berkshire hour of ten. The *Maybush* is a pleasant little pub and, since the elevation of its neighbour to the status of hotel, fulfils the function of the local. It has half a mile of fishing, and in this interest it resembles the second of the three *Trouts*, that at Tadpole bridge on a minor road to Bampton. This is the fishiest *Trout*: Fred Thacker recalled that at one time the *Trout* at Tadpole bridge was kept by A. Herring. The earliest reference to this bridge occurs in 1784, and it is possible that the *Trout* antedates it. For many years the keeper of Rushey lock was also the tenant of the *Trout*. The inn is small and pleasant, stone-flagged and full of stuffed fish, and retains its gas lighting. It

appears to have undergone no significant external alteration and
has a typical Cotswold air. Thacker recommended the cider and
the beer but warned against the claret cup; not that this would
affect many customers in the present day. The wharf at the *Trout*
was one of the old official public landing places, of which there
were only 6 in the 32 miles between Lechlade and Oxford.

More enormous embalmed fish can be found in the *Swan*, by the
oldest of the Thames bridges, Radcot. The river is divided into
two channels here; the navigable channel passes under the bridge
nearest to the *Swan*. It is the other bridge which is theancient one,
dating from the early thirteenth century. The socket into which a
cross fitted that stood above the central arch is still visible; there
is a legend that babies were once baptised in this makeshift font.
The *Swan*, after something of a fallow period, is in flourishing
condition; it is less harmonious architecturally than its neighbouring riverside pubs, but is an interesting building in a setting
spoiled only by the ubiquitous caravans.

Another of Thacker's favourite inns on the upper Thames was
the *Anchor* at Eaton Hastings. This was built in the eighteenth
century as the weir-keeper's house. Hart's Weir, as it came to be
called after a Mrs Hart who held the freehold in the early nineteenth century, was often complained of as being in bad condition; Mrs Hart herself was too poor to keep it in good repair. No
pound lock—the type found everywhere on our waterways—was
ever built here and, despite its ricketiness frequently referred to,
Hart's was the last of the Thames flash weirs to be removed, in
1937. The flash weir, precursor of the lock as we know it, was
constructed across the river to dam up the water to a certain
height; to permit the passage of a boat, stakes in the centre of the
weir could be drawn. Going upstream, the boat would have to be
hauled through the gap against the current; going downstream
the boat would be carried through by the 'flash' of water released.
In order to make them manageable it was often necessary to unload boats one side of the weir and reload them the other. The
flash released made its way down to the next weir, where the pro-
cedure was repeated. In 1826 it was estimated that a flash took 70
hours to travel from Lechlade to Sonning, including the delays at
the weirs en route— a speed of about 1mph.

Page 53
(*Above*) The *Trout*, Lechlade

(*Below*) The *Boat*, Ashleworth, River Severn

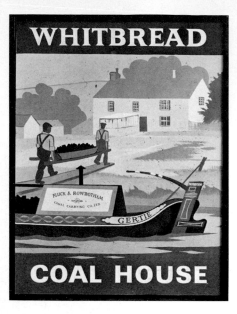

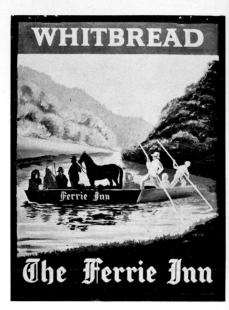

Page 54

(*Top left*) Sign of the *Coal House*, Apperley

(*Top right*) Sign of the *Ferrie Inn*, Symond's Yat

(*Bottom*) The *Three Locks*, Soulbury, Grand Union Canal

Hart's Weir was supplemented by a boatslide in 1911 when generally this stretch of river was usable only by light craft. Now this too has gone, and the site of Hart's Weir is marked by a foot-bridge, and by the *Anchor Inn*. The weir-keeper's house became a pub when an ale licence was granted for the bargemen; it is hard to see that there could have been other customers as there is no village or through road nearby. A full licence was granted after the war and the *Anchor* is now busy with a camp site adjacent and popular moorings. The little building by the footbridge, now serving as a shop, used to house a large collection of fishing tackle belonging to J. Jordan, a weir-keeper more concerned with angling than the upkeep of the navigation. At some time two bay windows have been added to the front but otherwise the *Anchor* has changed little and stands facing upstream towards the site of the weir and a lot nearer the water than most Thames-side pubs.

The last of the *Trouts*—which, like Godstow, has a religious ancestry—is at Lechlade, by St John's bridge. The first stone bridge here was erected in 1229 by the Prior; John Leland, the great antiquary, writing in the early sixteenth century remembered seeing 'at the very ende of St John's Bridge . . . a Chapelle in a Medow, and great enclosures of stone Waulles'. This was the Priory of St John the Baptist, which was dissolved in 1473. The *Trout Inn* was built as a hospice or almshouse attached to the Priory; after the dissolution it became an inn, known as the *Sygne of St John Baptist Head*. The name was changed to the *Trout* in 1704, Dame Hodson having kept it in its last years under the old title.

The old bridge, despite occasions when it fell into such dis-repair that it was dangerous to cross over it, endured until the early nineteenth century when it was replaced by the present one.

Lechlade's other bridge, Halfpenny Pike, so called because of the toll levied until 1839, was built in 1792, two years after St John's lock, the highest on the Thames. Both these constructions were consequences of the opening of the Thames & Severn Canal which locked into the river at Inglesham, half a mile above Lechlade, and brought increased trade to the town. Lechlade had been a busy enough inland port before then. In 1692 lively scenes are reported, with up to eight boats at one time loading at the

D

wharf with corn and cheese for London. There was sage cheese
and Cheshire cheese, brought down the Severn and Avon to
Tewkesbury and then transported by cart to the warehouses at
Lechlade. Goods also came upriver from London, were offloaded
and taken across to the Severn and thence by river to Bristol.
From Bristol ships sailed to Ireland, so the little town of Lechlade
was at the centre of a nationwide trading network. The *Trout* itself
figures in the Baskervile MS description:

> 'And because the meadow is surrounded with the river navigable
> from Oxford hither 'tis thick set with boats full of provisions
> brought from thence to entertain such people as come hither, and
> they go back with such goods as are bought at the fair to go down
> the stream. Here is hard by the bridge a very good inn for enter-
> tainment, and they have commonly strong march beer in bottles
> to sell, and pretty good wine, for as I remember in Leachlad there
> is no tavern.'

When the lock was opened William Wells was appointed keeper
for 3s 6d a week. Until 1830 it is probable that he and his successors
lived at the *Trout*, from which they fought an often losing battle
against the aggressive and blasphemous bargemen who objected
to having to pay tolls. In that year a lockhouse was built and the
Commissioners enforced their rule that lock-keepers should not
double as publicans and should live in the houses provided.

The *Trout* with its oak beams, stone-flagged bar and fine fireplace where legend says the monks once distilled Benedictine is a
handsome old house with a lawn running down to the weir,
shortly to be replaced by a less primitive, but probably uglier,
construction. It still holds the fishery rights to 2 miles of the river,
granted by Royal Charter to the brethren of the Priory some 700
years ago. The site of the Priory, a few yards from the inn, is now,
predictably perhaps, a caravan park.

4

RIVERSIDE 3
The Severn

To the motorist on the busy Gloucester–Chepstow road the *Bird in Hand* at Minsterworth looks a pleasant modern pub with a convenient car park and a view of the river—a good place from which to see the Severn Bore. This is, however, an old house modernised in 1939, and the only survivor of a run of six pubs along this bank of the Severn in a distance of about as many miles. Inside the present building the lines of the old house can be traced; under the wood block floor is the well from which the pub's water supply used to be drawn. A few inches under the lawn are the cobblestones of the original stable yard. The car park used to be a stone yard where stone, gravel and bricks for road-making and repairs were unloaded in the nineteenth century. The landlady of the time acted as the agent, paying the bargemen herself and collecting the money from the purchasers of the materials. The pub's 'Slate Book' records that in 1868 bricks cost sixpence a thousand and sand twopence a ton. The book also gives the prices of drinks at this time; cider was threepence a quart, ale twopence halfpenny a pint and old beer was threepence. A noggin of rum cost sevenpence and of gin sixpence, a noggin being a quarter of a pint. Tobacco was threepence an ounce. Many bills were allowed to run for months and were paid off in instalments.

Customers of the *Bird in Hand* included salmon fishermen who used to use a small brick and stone building known as the Fish House on the opposite bank to keep their gear and sleep in if necessary. The men fished half the width of the river by the long net method. A boat was stationed in the middle of the river with one man at the oars and another handling the net; two more men on the bank took the other end. The banks have been eroded in past years and the Fish House crumbled away and was eventually demolished in the 1950s. It used to be possible to walk across the river between Minsterworth and Elmore Back along an under-water ridge called Church Rock. A man could stand astride a gap in the ridge mid-stream and gaff a passing salmon beneath him, if he was brave enough and assured of his balance. At times the Rock used to be visible above water, but it has not been seen for many years.

Trows and barges navigated the Severn in the past, many of them penetrating the broad canals connecting with the river. The Stroudwater Canal left the Severn at Framilode, downstream from Minsterworth, and those trows which could lower their masts and rigging were able to voyage as far as the great inland port at Brimscombe, near Chalford in Gloucestershire, where goods could be transhipped into smaller vessels for the journey along the rest of the Thames & Severn Canal via Sapperton tunnel beneath the Cotswold escarpment and so to the Thames at Lechlade. A Severn trow in full sail is shown on one side of the halfpenny token issued at Brimscombe Port in 1795. The last stretch of the Thames & Severn Canal was abandoned in 1933 and the Stroud-water Canal was abandoned in 1954. Although Brimscombe Port has gone beyond recall there are promising plans to reopen the Stroudwater—as indeed there are to reopen another barge canal connecting with the Severn, the Droitwich, which used to serve the flourishing salt trade of that town.

The difficulties of navigating the Severn below Gloucester led to the construction of the Gloucester & Berkeley Canal, opened in 1827, a lockless navigation, except at its terminal points, with 16 swing bridges. Using the Bore, it could take as little as two hours to get from Sharpness to Gloucester, but it was a dangerous business and needed much experience and care. Without the Bore, or a strong tide, navigation upstream was impossible. Vessels might have to wait for weeks for enough depth of water to float them over shallows or rocks, or they would have to be unloaded and reloaded the other side of the obstacle if time was pressing. Hence the large number of pubs that used to line the river banks to provide refreshment or accommodation during long periods of inaction. As traffic moved on to the canal, many of these pubs lost the reason for their existence. However, there was still a use for the ferry houses and those like the *Bird in Hand* adjacent to a useful wharf. There was also for another 60 years after the opening of the canal a use for the *Shark* at Elmore Back. This small isolated cider house ran a profitable sideline in smuggling. The *Shark* was a posting-house for brandy and gin collected by barge from ships in the Bristol Channel and transported to London along with the cider barrels—a more exciting trade than the humdrum bricks, sand and stone of the *Bird in Hand*.

Most of today's Severnside inns have been rebuilt or modernised to some degree, but one that has so far escaped can be found a few miles upstream of Gloucester, at Ashleworth on the west bank of the river. Here there was an important ferry crossing as the towpath changed sides and the horses had to be taken across. The *Boat Inn* is a little cottage about 300 years old; it has one public room and the beer comes direct from the barrel. In front is a small terrace with cracked flagstones and the old brewhouse in one corner, the store room above it having been removed as it kept light from the cottage windows. The *Boat* is covered in creepers and there are flowers everywhere. With the decline in commercial traffic the river is silting up and the lane to the ferry point on the far side is almost indistinguishable. Not far from the *Boat* are the church, hall and a vast tithe barn that once belonged to the Priory of St Augustine in Bristol and is now in the care of the National Trust. The Priory built the stone quay and the lane leading to it alongside the *Boat*. A donkey-drawn barge used to work this stretch of river and if it was lucky enough to collect a tow the

donkeys would bring up the rear in a cock-boat of their own.
With the Cotswolds towering above, Ashleworth quay is a very
beautiful place.

North of Ashleworth is the first road crossing of the Severn
since Gloucester, at Haw bridge. Here is the *Haw Bridge Inn* with
an interesting sign showing the old and new bridges, and near to
it the *New Inn* also on the west bank. Upstream from Haw bridge
the *Coal House* at the end of a lane from Apperley has had its old
name restored in 1967, having been known as the *White Lion* for
many years. It is a solid squarish building of white-painted brick
facing the river. There was, as might be expected, a coal wharf
here and the pub was at one time the house of the wharfinger. The
coal came down river from Stourport, and hay was exported from
the wharf. Although at some distance from the village, the *Coal
House* is usually busy, being within easy driving distance of
Gloucester. The sign recalls its coal-trading past, even though the
name of the carrying company painted on the boat commemorates not a real company but the local schoolmaster and the
Engineer of the Severn River Board. At Chaceley is the *Yew Tree*,
a 400-year-old building not visually improved by recent extensions
and adjacent to a popular yacht club. Another old house is the
Lower Lode Hotel, as the river approaches Tewkesbury. The ferry
here stopped working about 25 years ago; now there is a slipway
and moorings for pleasure craft. There are also no fewer than ten
prohibitory notices telling the casual caller what he cannot do and
where he cannot do it; though to be fair these may contribute to
the well-kept appearance of the surroundings.

The Severn Bore on occasions has been noted as far north as
Worcester, where there is an old story that a man bathing was
killed by a swordfish. Between Tewkesbury and Worcester, with
the exception of Upton-on-Severn, there is a shortage of pubs.
The Danes outdid the Bore by penetrating as far up river as
Bevere, about 4 miles north of Worcester; close to Bevere lock and
weir is an inn called *Camp House*. Standing right on the river
bank it dates in part from the fifteenth century and looks like an
Elizabethan manor house in miniature. It was a staging post for
both coaches and barges. A nearby farm is called Retreat and the
pub remembers Camp Hill in its name—memories of Cromwell's

defeat of Prince Charles and the Scots in the Battle of Worcester, 1651. At the next bridge there is a pub on either bank: the *Holt Fleet* and, immersed in a caravan site, the *Wharf*. Next is the *Lenchford Hotel,* which marks the site of a ford. Then the last pub before Stourport, at the end of a potholed lane alongside the river. This is the *Hampstall Cider House,* a white painted brick building about 200 years old, the frontage spoiled by an obtrusive glass sun lounge. Here was another ferry crossing. The rowing boat ferry operated until 1960. Its larger predecessor ended its career in untimely manner in 1913 when it was swamped by a pleasure steamer cruising past on a Bank Holiday. Fourteen holidaymakers from Birmingham were drowned when the ferry sank; for two weeks, so it is said, their bodies lay unclaimed in an outbuilding of the pub while their relatives sought to avoid the expense of having them returned to Birmingham. There had been a ford here before the days of the ferry, and the pub had stabling for barge horses, presumably frequently used as there was a coal wharf only a few yards away. The stables are not likely to have been used before 1804 as the towing path to Worcester was not opened until that year. Manpower was the earlier form of traction, about 150 men being employed hauling boats between Coalbrookdale and Gloucester. A horse could do the work of six men, it was claimed; tolls were paid for nearly 400 horses in the mid-1820s, the busiest years for this kind of traffic.

A mile or so north of the *Cider House* is Lincomb lock, the uppermost lock on the river. Then come the sadly disused oil wharves of Stourport and the *Tontine Hotel* dominating the canal basins above the river on the town side. A shoal 2 miles above Stourport now marks the end of navigation on the Severn, which in former years had been regularly navigable as far up as Shrewsbury, extending to Welshpool when water levels permitted. With the opening of railways the upper reaches became less and less used; river traffic for Shrewsbury and above stopped in 1862 and for Bridgnorth in 1895. Bewdley, once a flourishing up-river port, lost its last barge trade in 1906.

What is one of the most interesting and historically significant stretches of the Severn is therefore no longer accessible by boat. This is the Ironbridge Gorge, a few miles above Bridgnorth, where the world's first iron bridge was constructed across the river in 1779. Here was one of the major growth points of the Industrial Revolution, the centre of the Shropshire iron industry. A great variety and number of trows, barges and boats plied on the river in the eighteenth and early nineteenth centuries carrying iron, coal and general merchandise, including the products of the Coalport China Works. The Ironbridge Gorge Museum Trust has now taken over responsibility for the industrial archaeology of the area, and at Blists Hill and Coalbrookdale the visitor can examine some of the monuments of our industrial prosperity. Opposite the *Swan* at Ironbridge the mid-nineteenth century Gothic warehouse, once used by the Coalbrookdale Company as a store for goods awaiting transfer to the trows, is to be turned into a museum of the river.

The *Swan* itself was once a warehouse, built between 1650 and 1700. It was converted to a public house shortly after the opening of the Iron Bridge, which had speedily become a tourist attraction. With stabling for eight horses and accommodation for four coachmen it seems likely that the *Swan* was intended to serve sightseers rather than the bargemen of the area. The *Tontine* is another house which had a similar function, 'being the place where the Traveller generally calls to regale, where he may be accommodated with carriage and horses; the house is commodious, & well built, situate at the end of the Iron Bridge:'—so it is pictured by the anonymous author of *A Description of Coalbrookdale in 1801*, published by the Museum Trust. The *White Hart* and the *Talbot*, the latter now closed, are also mentioned in this *Description*.

Jackfield, on the west bank of the river, was where those who derived employment from the Severn mostly lived. The *Black Swan* and the *Boat* survive from the river-trading days, but the *Severn Trow* and the *Tumbling Sailors* have gone. From contemporary accounts Jackfield must have been as lively, violent and dishonest a place as the average seaport of its day. Smuggling, poaching and general thievery were rife and the sailors fought their wives and tumbled their whores as if it was the Channel and not the Severn on which they earned their living. Jackfield also housed many bow hauliers, employed until the construction of the horse-towing paths to lug the vessels upstream, who were notorious for their dishonesty and immorality, although this is not surprising in view of the bestial nature of their occupation. Apart from the pubs there is little now in Jackfield to remind us of the bustling vigour of its past.

As well as the Iron Bridge and the Wood Bridge at Coalport there were several ferry crossings of the Severn. On the evening of 23 October 1799, the ferry from Jackfield to Coalport capsized in rough weather and 28 workers employed at John Rose's Coalport China factory were drowned, including several of the leading decorators. The Shropshire tub-boat canal ran past the China Works to a harbour near the Wood Bridge, although it did not connect directly with the river. A small pub, the *Shakespeare*, stands by the road in the angle between the course of the canal and the foot of the Hay inclined plane, which operated between 1793 and 1894 bringing the tub-boats in cradles up and down the incline from the canal's upper level 207ft above. The slope has been cleared by the Museum Trust and there are substantial visible remains of the docks at the top. The canal on the upper level is watered and has two recently rediscovered tub-boats floating on it. Running beneath the lower part of the incline is the Coalport Tar tunnel, the entrance to which is near the *Shakespeare* in what used to be the cellar of the village store. The Tar tunnel dates from 1787; it was the work of William Reynolds, the great Shropshire ironmaster, engineer and canal builder, who seems to have originally intended it as part of a canal scheme. It runs for some 1,000yd and may have connected with one of the shafts of the Blists Hill pits, though all the possibilities have not yet been explored. Liquid tar, or to be accurate natural bitumen, was struck about 300yd in. At first about 1,000gal a week were extracted, but the quantity diminished over the years and tar sales stopped in the 1840s. The Museum Trust has now taken over the tunnel and a length of it is open for inspection.

Apart from the bridge there is plenty to see in Ironbridge Gorge, including of course the Coalbrookdale site itself where the first Abraham Darby smelted iron ore with coke, both obtained in the locality, and where the third Abraham Darby cast the girders to make the bridge. From the *Swan* downriver to the *New Passage Hotel* the Severnside inns are indicators of the river's rich and varied history. Via the river the products of Coalbrook-dale travelled down to Gloucester, Chepstow and Bristol, and the pubs that have been mentioned with others beside—the *Stone Bench* at Elmore, the *Salmon* at Elmore Back, the *Berkeley Arms* by the one time cattle-crossing at Purton, and the isolated *New Inn*, or *Windbound*, at Sheperdine, where vessels could tie up inside the sea wall and the crews could drink until they could drink no more—were all there for the purpose of serving the river traffic. From many of them, however, the opening of the canal from Sharpness to Gloucester drew the trade away and now there is only a handful that can welcome customers arriving by boat.

The canal has its own selection of pubs, including two over-looking the docks at Sharpness, one of which, the *Severn Bridge and Railway*, shows on its sign the single-track railway bridge over the river. On to a pier of this bridge two tankers were swept by the tide on an October night in 1960. Two spans of the bridge fell; the tankers caught fire and five men were lost. Some years later the bridge was dismantled, and the hotel sign is one of its few memorials.

North of Sharpness at Purton the *Berkeley Hunt* stands by the lower swing bridge, not far from the *Berkeley Arms* overlooking the river. A farmhouse before the canal opened, the *Berkeley Hunt* became a boatmen's pub in the 1830s. Despite, or perhaps because of, the violent hunting scenes on its wallpaper, the *Berkeley Hunt* is a pleasant and inviting pub. Neither of the two public rooms has a bar; one has a large black settle, and both an atmosphere which can only be described as homely. Drinks are served from a counter in the central passage; there is a friendly simplicity about this inn from which 'modernisation' could only detract.

The next pub north of Purton is at Shepherd's Patch, near the Slimbridge Wildfowl Trust which lies between the river and the canal. Four miles on is Saul junction, where there is a waterway crossroads with the Stroudwater Canal.

The northernmost pub on the canal is the *Pilot* at Sellars bridge, near Hardwicke. It stands four-square on an embankment, facing across to one of the attractive Grecian temple style bridge-keeper's houses which are characteristic of the dignity of this waterway. A short distance north of the *Pilot* is an oil wharf, now the terminus of the canal's oil traffic. MV *Bude* is one of the five tankers which call here, one every two or three days. She is 211ft long and 30ft beam, edging through the bridges with a few inches to spare. 1,000 tons of high octane fuel is the usual cargo. These vessels apart, there is little commercial traffic on the canal nowadays, but grain, timber and granite setts do find their way to Gloucester docks by barges and the occasional coaster. There are some remarkable dockside warehouse buildings; now that the planners have done their work in the centre of the city, Gloucester docks are second only to the cathedral and its immediate surroundings for architectural and visual interest.

5

RIVERSIDE 4
Chepstow to York

∽∽∽∽∽∽∽∽∽∽∽∽∽∽∽∽∽∽∽∽∽∽∽∽∽∽∽∽∽∽∽∽∽∽

One ought to mention inns alongside some of the other rivers which have through the centuries contributed to the country's trading prosperity. The Wye, most glorious of rivers, carried trading vessels from medieval times until the beginning of the twentieth century, although little immediate evidence presents itself to the tourist 'doing the Wye Valley' today. You may find one piece of evidence if you pass through Bristol on your way, in the name of the fine old pub in King Street, the *Llandoger Trow*. Llandoger is correctly Llandogo, a village on the west bank of the Wye between Chepstow and Monmouth, and the Trow of course was the characteristic sailing vessel of the neighbouring river Severn and of the Lower Wye. Llandogo itself has its reminder in the name of the *Sloop Inn*. For centuries Chepstow was a port and an important shipbuilding centre; it still preserves just a trace of its maritime past. The industrial development of the late sixteenth century brought wire and copper works and a paper mill to the riverside, and from wharves were shipped the coal and iron of the Forest of Dean. Monmouth in the eighteenth century was principally dependent on the river for transport; for a time the river was navigable above Hereford to which place gangs of men had to haul the barges until a towpath was constructed in 1809. Pigot's *Directory for Monmouthshire*, 1835, describes Chepstow as 'one of the finest places for launching vessels in the kingdom'; at that time along The Back by the river there were eight public houses, including the *Steam Packet* and the *Sailors' Tavern*. Monmouth, according to Pigot, 'enjoys a trade with Bristol and other places by means of the Wye, and imports groceries and various goods necessary for the consumption of a large tract of inland country; and, by the same means of transition, a considerable exportation of timber and bark is carried on'. In Weir Head Street, where the barge-masters lived, there was a pub called the *Brockwear Boat*. Brockweir, on the Gloucestershire bank a few miles below Monmouth, was the last village to be served by trows at the beginning of the century. There are indications of the old quayside here—with the *New Inn* a few yards away up the hill—and at Tintern. Here the Abbey, superb even in its decay, draws the sightseers, catered for by a handful of hotels and inns of varying degrees of sophistication. The most charming of the Wyeside pubs, however, is on the Monmouthshire bank higher up, opposite the village of Redbrook, itself not so long ago an industrial centre with a tinplate works and a bridge carrying a tramroad incline over the road leading up to the Forest. This pub is the *Boat*, a small, old, white cottage under the shadow of a railway bridge now, the track removed, relegated to a mere footbridge over the river. The *Boat* is at the lowest point of a loop road that twists and slides precipitately down from the hills above; water trickles down the rocks beside the inn and there was a cherry tree on the river bank in front. The *Boat* is at least two centuries old, possibly much more; but no one locally seems to know anything of its history. Unfortunately the interior has suffered from ill-judged attempts to cater for modern tastes; of all pubs in which to find a juke-box this seems the most unlikely, and the most unsuitable.

The last of Monmouth's riverside pubs was demolished a few years ago. Upstream there is no shortage at Symond's Yat, an old ferry crossing where now boat trips are a popular attraction. Pleasure boating was indeed popular on the Wye for many years; the poet Thomas Gray was one among many who regarded a voyage on the river as the 'principal feature' of a tour of the Wye Valley. Ross was the usual starting point; the wild, romantic scenery attracted men of taste and letters. Wrote one traveller: 'Endless varieties discover at every turn something new and unexpected; so that we are at once amused and surprised, and curiosity is constantly gratified but never satiated.' And this river meant much to another, greater writer:

> O sylvan Wye! thou wanderer through the woods,
> How often has my spirit turned to thee!

Perhaps no other river is as inspiring, in a literary sense, as the Wye, although the lower reaches of the Medway greatly attracted Charles Dickens, as did the tidal Thames. Allington lock is the dividing line between the Lower Medway, today again a busy commercial river, and the upper river, popular with pleasure traffic. The *Malta Inn* by the lock reflects both aspects of the river. It was built in 1784 as a pub for bargemen and quarrymen. Nearby is *Gibraltar House*, which also used to be a bargemen's inn although it is no longer licensed. In 1966 the *Malta* was adapted to cope with the increasing demands of the cruisers and to capitalise on its riverside setting to encourage diners-out. It is now most luxurious, a far remove from the days of the press gangs who plagued, harried and impressed the bargemen, so much so that the navigation company pointed out indignantly that their activities were hindering the supplying of timber to the dockyards for the vessels which the barge crews were being carried off to man.

Commercial traffic on the River Wey, navigable for 19½ miles from Godalming to Thames lock at Weybridge, ended in 1969. The Wey was once part of an ambitious line from London to Portsmouth which was open throughout for only a few years in the 1820s. This line also incorporated the Wey & Arun Junction and the Portsmouth & Arundel canals; the latter did not operate for long, but the Wey & Arun endured until 1871. In 1964 the Wey Navigation was given by Mr H. W. Stevens to the National

Trust, who had owned and traded on it for many years. The remaining length of the river to Godalming was given to the Trust 4 years later. Between Weybridge and Guildford there is a handful of pubs at which boats can moor. There is the *Pelican* at Weybridge and the *Anchor* at Pyrford lock; the *Anchor* was an old bargemen's inn until the 1930s, when it was rebuilt and extended. The *New Inn* at Send is by the towpath. On the approach to Guildford, at Stoke, is another one-time bargemen's inn, the *Row Barge*, although its character has changed considerably in recent times.

By comparison with Wey and Medway the Trent is an enormous river, looping around the centre of England and navigable for almost a hundred miles. As a navigation both Romans and Danes used its waters; as a trading river in the nineteenth century it was the main line connecting seven other navigations from the Trent & Mersey Canal to the Sheffield & South Yorkshire, and on to the Humber and the other Yorkshire rivers and canals. Today for purposes of commercial transport it is an under-used, or unused, asset, awaiting the dawn of a new Age of Enlightenment; which needs to come before the whole of the Midlands is turned into one vast Spaghetti Junction.

The Trent has few locks—about a dozen—but has been comparatively slow to attract pleasure traffic in its lower reaches in tidal waters. Many people are finding that with confidence and care it does not prove too intimidating, and those interested in trying it should read Fred Doerflinger's account in *Slow Boat Through Pennine Waters*, which gives an up-to-date description of a voyage through its length. Alongside the river there seem to be fewer pubs than power stations, despite the predominantly rural scenery. There are two pubs by the junction with the Erewash Canal; the *Navigation* is riverside, but the *Fisherman's Rest* is an Erewash pub, built by the canal company in 1791 as the *Erewash Navigation Inn*. There are plenty of pubs in Nottingham, where the navigation uses a stretch of the Nottingham Canal, including the ancient and very well known *Trip to Jerusalem*. Unhappily the Nottingham Canal is nothing for the city to be particularly proud of in its present condition.

Farther north at the old ferry crossing at Stoke Bardolph is the

Ferry Boat Inn; ferry crossings were the reasons for the existence of most of the Trent's pubs. For examples there are the *Anchor* at Gunthorpe and the *Elm Tree* at Hoveringham, not forgetting the enormous *Star & Garter* at the Hazleford ferry crossing near Bleasby. Most of these ferries date from the Middle Ages; none of them operates today except at Farndon, south of Newark. There is a pub here too, the *Britannia*. Newark itself has no actual riverside pubs, which provides an excuse to moor and explore this fascinating town with one of the best market squares in the country. There is still some waterborne trade to Newark. Northwards only the *Newcastle Arms* at North Muskham stands by the river before Cromwell lock is reached and the beginning of the tidal navigation. Then for miles there are few bridges, the villages keep clear of the flood plain, and occasional power stations loom up on each side. The Fossdyke comes in from the east; then the Chesterfield Canal at Stockwith from the west, the basin providing a safe mooring and the *Crown Inn*. The next junction is with the Stainforth & Keadby Canal, with the *Friendship Inn* at Keadby junction often used by the crew of commercial vessels while waiting for the tide. This pub used to provide refreshment and stabling for the canal boats as well, but the stables have been converted into a dance hall and the canal could use more trade. From Keadby it is less than 10 miles to Trent Falls, where the Trent flows into the Humber. The Trent is a lowland river by nature; the movement of the water is often the most exciting sight to see. Its tributaries, Dove and Derwent, flow through more dramatic scenery. It is worth noting that when Daniel Defoe undertook his *Tour* in the 1720s the principal commodity the Trent then carried was Cheshire cheese, about 4,000 tons a year of it being brought by the river from Burton to Hull and thence distributed over the eastern counties of the kingdom.

From Trent Falls eastward is the Humber estuary, westward the Yorkshire Ouse winding past Whitgift, where the *Ferry House* marks the site of a once much used crossing, Goole, with its fascinating collection of dockside taverns in varying states of decay, through Selby and on to York. York's river trade has sadly declined, but the riverside has many fine warehouses and is still an integral part of the city. It seems to be waiting for the

Page 71
(*Top*) The *Grand Junction Arms*, Southall, from a painting of about 1880; (*Centre*) The *Boat*, Loughborough; (*Bottom*) The *Greyhound*, Hawkesbury junction

(*Top*) *The Big Lock*, Middlewich, Trent & Mersey Canal; (*Centre*) The *Old Broken Cross*, Northwich, Trent & Mersey Canal; (*Bottom*) The *Berkeley Hunt*, Purton, Gloucester & Berkeley Canal

vessels to come once more. In the 1830s it took 33 hours to travel by water from York to London; three river steamers plied to Hull, with connection by coastal steamers to London. The fare was 11 shillings for a saloon, or 7 shillings for a fore-cabin. On the wall of the *Ousebridge Inn* are marked the flood levels, going back to 1824. The highest level was recorded in 1947, with 1897 as the runner-up. This is a pleasant, straightforward little pub; the date 1898 over the door is of course no indication of its real age. It would appear from the overhanging top storey that the building is at least partly seventeenth century, certainly older than the present Ouse bridge, completed in 1820, which replaced an earlier bridge of 1565. There is a horrifying story that the *Ousebridge* is to be modernised in the style of a Tyrolean mountain chalet, or something equally inappropriate. Modernisation or conversion are by no means necessarily evil; there is a good example of a successful effort above the bridge where a warehouse has been converted into the *Tavern in the Town*, a large pub with a number of dining-rooms. This is both interesting and imaginative; in other cities such a building might well have been demolished to be replaced by the starkness of concrete and glass. The *Ousebridge* is on King's Staithe, opposite the Old Crane wharf, the very centre of York's commercial activity in centuries past. If it is necessary to attract more tourists to the pub—and brewers should not be expected to be more altruistic than other trades—then why not capitalise on the character of the area by making use of the traditions of the past in a renovation scheme rather than by using alien gimmickry? But perhaps it is only a rumour and it may never happen after all.

6

CANALSIDE
'This wretched life'

~~~~~~

Canal traffic was at its peak around the year 1830. Nearly all the major lines had been completed and railway competition was hardly yet thought of. There were nearly 1,000 miles of navigable waterway in England and Wales. Several of the older-established canal companies were paying dividends of over 40 per cent. At a rough estimate, about 100,000 men were employed on the canals and at their locks, wharves and warehouses.

It was in 1830 that Parliament amended the 1828 Licensing Act. The 1830 Act empowered publicans to take out beer licences without applying to the magistrates, and it abolished the duty on beer. The result of this measure, intended to benefit the working-classes by providing them with cheaper and better beer, was an immediate and sensational increase in the number of beerhouses; within 6 years over 40,000 new ones were opened. Beer prices fell and there was at first a sharp drop in the consumption of spirits. This did not last, however; it was not long before the gin producers fought back and soon the gin palace, providing facilities which the humble beerhouse could not match, became a common sight in the poorer areas of industrial towns. But along the routes of the canals the beer-houses continued to flourish. Subsequent legislation, under

The *King's Lock*, Middlewich, Trent & Mersey Canal

pressure from the temperance movement, introduced some control, but this was the century of free enterprise and law was not always closely observed. In *Our Canal Population*, published in 1875, George Smith wrote:

> 'Public houses of the lowest kind are along the sides of the canal. There the men, women and children are to be seen at all hours of the day, and fighting, ruffianism, and blackguardism of the worst kind are indulged in.'

Smith, usually distinguished as 'of Coalville' in Leicestershire, was one of the breed of vigorous nineteenth-century Nonconformist reformers. After persuading Parliament to pass an Act regulating the working conditions of children in the brickyards, he turned his attention to the living conditions of the canal boat people. His publicity campaign led to the passing of the Canal Boats Act in 1877. Disappointed at the ineffectiveness of this legislation because of the lack of any compulsive element, Smith continued his campaign in *Canal Adventures by Moonlight*, 1881, and was rewarded by a second

Canal Boats Act 3 years later which remedied many of the defects of
the first and resulted in a general improvement of the conditions
of life on the family boats. That there was much that needed improvement goes without question. Smith quotes a remark made to
him by a boatman at Paddington, that 'the boatman who first put a
woman into a boat cabin deserved hanging', and himself refers to
the living accommodation on the boats as 'those hot, damp, close,
stuffy, buggy, filthy, and stinking holes, commonly called boat
cabins'.

To George Smith, and to others of the time, the canalside pub
was a place of much horror. It was frequently met with too; near
Braunston on the Grand Junction there were ten pubs in a stretch of
1 mile. In March, 1875, the *Birmingham Daily Mail* published a
description of a typical canalside pub:

You come on it suddenly, hiding modestly in a dark hole or corner
of a dark wall. Its dirty little windows display weird and fearful
compounds; its sign hints in irregular printing 'ale, porter, cider,
and tobacco,' and being 'drunk on the premises.' I go . . . to
inspect the amphibious public. I find the grimiest of low-ceilinged
taprooms, a truly savage and barbaric 'tap' wherein is dispensed
the thinnest and flattest beer I have ever yet come across. This is
the 'bargee's' usual tipple, for rum is only a special drink for great
occasions. Greasy wooden 'settles' and battered wooden tables
furnish the apartment, and there come the 'jolly bargemen' to make
merry. The walls have two distinct and clearly defined rows of
black lines, indicating the presence of greasy backs and heads, and
when the boatmen have mustered 'harmony' reigns. . . . The
ballads peculiar to boatmen possess either the humour of the not
specially decorous country ditty, or the sentimentality of the Holywell street 'lay'. . . . Occasionally the younger boatmen launch out
into a sadly garbled version of some flashy music-hall song, but
this is looked upon rather coldly. The singer having duly rammed
his hands deeply into his breeches pockets, leans his head against
the wall, fixes his eyes on the ceiling, and goes to work with the
air of a man doing penance for his sins. The choruses are frequent
and tremendous. The 'harmony' is often relieved by a little step
dancing, in which, strange to say, the boatman is an adept; the big,
burly men are wonderfully light of foot, and keep time accurately.
The orchestra is usually composed of a fearfully dilapidated old
man, operating feebly on the last remains of an ancient fiddle, and
extracting thence wheezing jigs and ghastly strains of nigger

'breakdowns'. I confess that I incline to look with much horror on the boatman's 'public'. These are places so retired and hidden that what can be easier than a little quiet drinking within prohibited hours, or keeping open later than Mr Cross approves of? They are nasty, suspicious dens, to say the least of it, and I fear that the over-refreshed 'bargee' is by no means a lamb when he gets home to his unfortunate family.

In the manner of many of his contemporaries, the Birmingham journalist makes no attempt to conceal his social and cultural superiority. To the family boatman the canalside pub must have been a haven of refuge from the overcrowded cabin and the wailing of innumerable children. But it seems clear that by the 1870s boatmen were not particularly favoured customers in many public houses. Smith was told that there was a time when they were put into the parlour for their drink, but 'now they are kicked and cuffed about anywhere, and put in any dirty hole out of sight, and the drink they get is not of the best sort'. And John Hollingshead complained about the 'thin, sour beer' which was all he could get to drink in the pubs along the Grand Junction during his trip to Birmingham some years earlier. The boatman's 'fourpenny'—fourpence a quart—was described by George Smith as tasting 'like a decoction of saltpetre, vinegar, treacle and mint'.

Smith himself tramped many miles along the towpaths investigating the working of the first Canal Boats Act, and in his second book he gave a description of a visit he paid to the *Black Boat*, a real boatman's public house near Bull's bridge, Southall. From the outside he found it moderately prepossessing: 'a square, detached villa of more than a century old.' The gate was locked, so he went round to what he thought was the stable-yard for the boat horses, where he discovered a crowd of boatmen and their families all looking extremely dirty. One of them showed him in to what at first he thought was the stable under the upper rooms. Here he was met by 'a coarse, bloated, vulgar, dirty-looking boatwoman, whose face seemed to be almost the colour of a piece of raw beef a week old'. He asked her to show him the way upstairs, where he could get some bread, cheese and ginger beer, but was told that there wasn't any upstairs so in the stable he had to stay. He sat down and took stock of his surroundings:

The fireplace consisted of a few iron bars and bricks; the walls had been devoid of the plaster in many places, and the beauty of rough 'London stacks' drawn out of the piles with crowbars could be seen as if they had been thrown together by a jerry builder with a shovel. [Having at one time been manager of a brickyard, Smith knew about this sort of thing.] Various colours and hues and tints were observable upon the wall, which had been derived from the boatmen's habiliments according to the cleanliness, thickness, or colour of the dirt upon them, i.e. a boatman engaged upon a 'flour boat' would leave a white mark upon the settle where he had been sitting to enjoy his 'fourpenny'; a boatman engaged in the coal trade would leave his black mark; and in like manner would those engaged in the London sewage and Birmingham gas-tar business. . . . There were several poor boat children in the place, who seemed to enjoy the 'fourpenny' quite as well as either the men or the women. Of course the little boat children had not legs long enough to cause them to leave impress upon the settle, consequently their tiny marks were left upon the floor as they toddled and paddled about upon the mosaic pavement of stone and brick ends, which very often were not quite pleasant, and as easy to remove as the stains from the settles. Cobwebs could be seen by the hundred hanging down from the ceiling. My bread, cheese and ginger beer were handed to me from a kind of beggar's pantry, such as I have seen in Drury Lane, and placed upon a table not as white as snow. While I was crumbling my bread and cheese and drinking my ginger beer from the neck of the bottle, in came two other boat-women, with several children, whose language was so disjointed that I could with great difficulty understand what they were talking about. Before I left this specimen of English civilisation, I gave an old boatman, who looked half-starved, some coppers to purchase a loaf with, but instead of doing so he called for a quart of 'fourpenny', which he drank without taking his mouth from the jug; wiping his mouth on his coat sleeve he said 'Thank you, sir, thank you, sir,' and there was an end of it.

There seems reason to believe that canalside pubs may in general have been at their least salubrious in the period when these accounts were written. Boatmen's wages were poor, and for many years the industry had been contracting under pressure from railway competition. For reasons of economy many boatmen had brought their families to live with them on the boats, but until George Smith became concerned no one from the outside world showed any interest in their living conditions, their health or the education of

their children. Smith prints a poem which he says was sent to him
by a man who had lived for 20 years by a canal basin:

> Mother dear, I am so weary,
> Weary of this wretched life;
> Sailing, driving, always boating!
> Can I see a better life?
> See those flowers in yonder garden,
> And those happy children play;
> Here are we shut in this cabin,
> Small and crowded, night and day.
>
> Mother dear, O, can you tell me
> Why it is we're living so?
> Father, mother, sisters, brothers,
> Nine in all, as you well know,
> Ever floating on the water
> Midst the curse of wicked men,
> Wretched, cruel, fierce, drunken;
> Could I never sail again!

It is true that there are reports of happy families with clean and
healthy children, living in brightly painted cabins, and sometimes
owning a canalside cottage as well. But there is too much evidence
on the other side for it to be thought that these are anything more
than exceptions helping to prove the rule. To a great extent—and
more so probably in the years before the recent run of mergers and
takeovers in the brewery trade—the public house reflects taste and
preferences of its principal customers. And when these customers
have only a pittance to spend, the lowest common denominator is
likely to determine the standard.

7

CANALSIDE 1
The Grand Union Canal

~~~~~~

The Grand Union Canal as we know it today is the result of the amalgamation of several canal companies over the years. The most important element is the line of the Grand Junction, from Thames lock at Brentford to Braunston junction. There are about 25 pubs along this 93-mile waterway; but in the 1870s there were 10 within a single mile near Braunston. The survivors, however, reflect clearly the varied origins of the canalside pub. Their histories are at a long remove from the glamorous stories of the great coaching inns; not even those that antedate the canal ever provided a bed for Queen Elizabeth I or a refuge for an escaping Charles Stuart. The nearest we get to literary history is in the pages of *Household Words*, the weekly journal edited by Charles Dickens which appeared in the 1850s.

John Hollingshead, later to become manager of the Gaiety Theatre and the man who introduced the can-can to English audiences, undertook a voyage from London to Birmingham as a passenger in the fly-boat *Stourport* and published an account of his experiences in *Household Words* in 1858. Much of it he enjoyed but his search for food and drink along the way was not always

profitable. As they travelled north, he and his companion walked
ahead of the boats, looking for refreshment.

> At last we reached a melancholy canalside tavern; where nothing
> was to be got but a very thin and sour ale, and where we were given
> to understand, in answer to our anxious enquiries, that in those
> parts the common barn-fowl was a bird almost as scarce as the
> celebrated dodo.
>
> On again we walked, with increasing appetites and decreasing
> hopes, until we came upon the village of Stoke Brewin. . . .where
> we found another foodless tavern stocked with the thin, sour ale;
> and as the *Stourport* and its butty-barge had not yet arrived, we
> entered the pale of mild dissipation to drink ourselves into a better
> humour.
>
> 'I suppose Lundun be very dool now?' inquired the young lady
> who served us with the beer.
>
> 'Dull!' almost shouted Cuddy, whose gallantry was quite gone:
> 'the dullest street in the dullest part of the city, at the dullest time
> of the day, and the dullest part of the year, is a bear garden com-
> pared with Stoke Brewin!'

To the mid-Victorian Londoners Stoke Bruerne may well have
seemed thus. Hollingshead can hardly have foreseen that in a little
over a century it would become a highly popular resort, with the
Waterways Museum (in his time a mill building) drawing tens of
thousands of visitors annually. About 12 years after his visit, the
'foodless tavern'—the *Boat*—passed into the hands of the Wood-
ward family, who have run it ever since. Since then—if it was not so
before—it has become one of the best-liked and best-known of all
canal pubs. The building probably dates from the seventeenth
century and was originally three cottages, of which one became the
village beerhouse. It became called the *Boat* when the canal opened
in 1805, and was reorientated, as it were, for the convenience of its
new customers. The cottages adjoining became a butcher's shop
and a dairy, and were eventually incorporated in the pub. Adjacent
were stabling and a hut for the men employed to leg the boats
through Blisworth tunnel. Many of the early canalside buildings at
Stoke Bruerne remain, although the functions of some of them
have changed.

The *Boat* is an attractive thatched house. Being a free house it has
been spared some of the disfigurements of external advertising, and

apart from its own sign it carries on its outside wall a plaque of the Birmingham Fire Insurance. Inside in the inner bar there is an old rough-hewn round red oak table, which used to rotate. A favourite boatman's joke was to distract the attention of one of their number and then swing the table so that his beer passed to his neighbour. The resulting language and fisticuffs caused the previous landlord to

The *Admiral Nelson*, Braunston, Grand Union Canal

immobilise it. It is said that it was on this table that the bodies of two men badly injured in a collision in the tunnel were laid in 1861. A more typical occasion in the *Boat* is recalled by Tim Wilkinson who, with his ex-fashion model wife, became a working boatman for a while in the last days of commercial traffic after World War II. He recalls a splendid evening, drinking and playing dominoes, 'and music from an accordion, really well played by an old boater with a long flowing white moustache and smart navy-blue trilby hat, which he raised every time we clapped his tunes. We sang sad old songs like "Goodbye Old Ship of Mine" . . .' The Woodwards used to have their own narrow boats, and the *Boat*, with this long family connection, with its photographs of Sister Mary Ward who lived opposite and was the beloved nurse and friend of boat families for decades, and with the memories of Jack James, sometime a Number One on the Grand Union, lock-keeper and initiator of the Waterways Museum, is a part of canal history.

We left John Hollingshead and his friend complaining about Stoke Bruerne. Things improved for them as they travelled north. Near Braunston they came to a boatmen's village, a few houses round a lock with a bootmaker and a tailor and hosier catering only for boatmen, with a window full of bright blue thick worsted stockings and fustian trousers hanging up outside. Rrefreshment was available too:

> Close to the lock-gates was a long, low-roofed tavern, grocer's and butcher's all in one, kept by a female relation of our commander. We left the barge in a body . . . to try the strength and flavour of the tavern's best ale. We entered a long room, with a very low ceiling, old diamond-paned, leaden-framed windows, containing seats, an enormous kitchen-range, clean deal kitchen-tables, and a tall clock in a mahogany case like a small wardrobe. Through a door at the end was seen the grocery department, communicating with, and terminating in, the butcher's shop. The passage formed such a tempting vista of food that we could not delay a moment, and, leaving the boatmen to drink their ale, we rushed through and immediately purchased several pounds of beefsteak . . .

It is possible that the pub referred to is the *Admiral Nelson*, just over half way down the Braunston flight of locks. But four pubs have vanished between here and the *New Inn*, at the top of Buckby locks on the south side of Braunston tunnel, and Hollingshead's pub may have been one of these. The *Nelson Inn*, as it used to be known, is certainly an old building; its history can be traced back to 1730 and it may be a hundred years older than that. It was originally a farm-house, until the farmer turned to selling beer to boatmen when the canal opened and it was known as a public house in the early nineteenth century. It is interesting to note in passing that the pub with two cottages and over 2 acres of land was sold in 1930 for £600, and in 1936 for £900. Unfortunately the records do not show who owned the pub in 1858. The commander of Hollingshead's craft was Captain Randle, but the female connection cannot be established. In any event, the *Nelson* is a pleasant, unpretentious old canal pub, where you can always hear news of the happenings on the cut.

As mentioned, the *New Inn* is now the next pub south of the

Admiral Nelson. Another old house, this closed a few years ago leaving no pubs at all on the Buckby flight where once there used to be five. Happily it has been reopened, now elegant with antique furniture, and seems to be justifying the confidence of its new owners. But the *Crown and Anchor, Boat, Three Horseshoes* and *Spotted Cow* have gone for ever, as well as three more at the old Buckby wharf, together with a brewery. Southwards apart from the *Narrow Boat* by A5 at Weedon there is nothing until the *Boat* at Stoke Bruerne. On this length there were about seven pubs in the past. The sign of one, the *Navigation* at Gayton, is preserved in the Waterways Museum, and the *Sun and Moon*—with Stars added since—is a cafe in Blisworth.

South of Stoke Bruerne there is a long publess stretch. Cosgrove has the *Navigation Inn* at Castlethorpe wharf and the old *Barley Mow*, another one-time farmhouse, in the village, accessible from the towpath by a miniature tunnel under the canal. The nearest pub to Wolverton aqueduct is the *Galleon*, popular with fishermen. Hereabouts the new city of Milton Keynes is creeping over the landscape, and the character of the clientele of the *Black Horse* at Great Linford is likely to change. This unspoiled house with its brown panelled bar seems to be tucked in beside the canal but antedates it by at least a century. Its licence goes back to 1727. It has kept much of its stabling, and is attractive outside as in. At Linford wharf, a few hundred yards away, there used to be another attractive inn, the *Old Wharf*, near the junction with the Newport Pagnell Canal which closed in 1863 and of which there are few traces left. The *Old Wharf*, a simple but dignified building, closed as a pub in 1963.

One of the intriguing featues of conversation with canal people is that they often refer to places of importance which mean practically nothing to anyone else. One such place is Fenny—Fenny Stratford. This has been consumed by Bletchley, but the *Red Lion* by lock and swing bridge remains indisputably Fenny. This lock has a rise of only a foot and was built as a temporary measure in 1802 in order to lower the pound to northward which suffered badly from leakage. The problem was solved, but the Grand Junction Company never found themselves able to afford to remove the lock afterwards. When in order to help accelerate traffic and economise on water the locks between Stoke Bruerne and Stoke Hammond were duplicated in the 1830s, Fenny Stratford was the only exception. The *Red Lion* is mentioned as existing in 1871, the occupant being also a grocer. It was rebuilt in 1901, and is very much of a canal pub; it is hardly noticeable from the road. It was a favourite meeting place for boatmen and has good examples of their painted ware on display. The *Red Lion* is something of a contrast to the next canalside pub southwards, the *Three Locks* at Soulbury, originally the *New Inn*, near Stoke Hammond. This stands beside the bottom lock, but draws a heavy trade from the busy main road parallel to the canal. In the past few years the Victorian brick exterior has been concealed beneath white cement and the interior has been re-modelled to produce one large room only, a move destructive of individual character. Only some odd-shaped windows are re-minders of the earlier idiosyncrasies of the building. At the *Three Locks* George Smith stopped for ginger beer, sprats and bread and cheese on 31 December 1878, and counted twelve unregistered boats passing through the locks while he ate.

The *Globe Inn* near Leighton Buzzard provides another contrast. Built in the sixteenth century it was a smallholding which became a beerhouse to serve the navvies when the canal was being cut. It stands isolated on a rural stretch of towpath but never became a regular boatman's pub, possibly because there is no lock close at hand. There were stables attached to the house which were converted in 1969 to make an extra bar. The *Globe* led a quiet life until lately but its popularity with motorists has become such that a car park to take 130 vehicles has now been made.

Marsworth, by the junction with the Aylesbury arm, has two popular *Lions*, a *Red* and a *White*. The canal's original name is remembered, not for the only time, at Bulbourne, where the *Grand Junction Arms* faces the British Waterways workshops where lock gates are made. Built in 1852 the *Grand Junction* was rebuilt after a fire some years later; it became temporarily notorious when two gamekeepers were shot and killed nearby and the poachers' guns were discovered in the canal beside. This house was often used as an overnight stop by boat crews who stabled their horses in the barn and the present cellar. Near to Tring, this used to be Rothschild country and the land on which the pub stands was once owned by the family. In 1896 a scale model of the Foxton inclined plane was constructed at Bulbourne and led to the installation at Foxton itself, a considerable engineering feat which unfortunately never met the success it deserved.

The canal is now on its summit level across the Chilterns. The descent to London begins at Cowroast lock, near Wiggington. The *Cow Roast Inn* is beside the road, a few yards from the canal. John Hassell in his *Tour of the Grand Junction Canal*, 1819, described it as 'a respectable little inn'. He continues:

> This spot I should conceive, to be most erroneously named. It is famed for the richest pasturage. The meadows on the sides of the Grand Junction are luxuriant in the extreme, and during the dreadful drought in August last year, 1818, the whole of the Cow Roast valley was in a state of the most fertile vegetation. Here we saw herds of cows grazing, and observed a fresh drove of sucklers with their calves coming up to remain for the night, and we found, upon enquiry, that this inn was one of the regular stations for the drovers halting their cattle for refreshment; hence I should suppose, the proper name is the Cow Rest, or resting place of those animals . . .

The pub indeed was once called the *Cow Rest* and was used by the drovers from the Midlands and North Wales on their way to London. It was also popular with the boatmen who could obtain food there after their long climb through 56 locks from Brentford. The name of the pub is recorded as the *Cow* in 1806. The building is about 320 years old and is said always to have been a pub. It has been extended and modernised but the pattern of the small drinking rooms can be discerned as the intervening structural beams have been retained. Hassell mentions two cottages by the lock known as Water-gauge houses, in one of which 'a person placed there by the Duke of Northumberland' lived in order to check with an employee of the canal company that the same quantity of water allowed by the company to the millers, for whom the Duke was trustee, above the lock was returned to the canal below.

So far, the pubs on the Grand Union have been infrequent, but at Berkhamsted there are three within a quarter of a mile along the towpath. The *Crystal Palace* succeeded an earlier beerhouse; it was built in 1854, inspired by the Great Exhibition 3 years previous. The entire gable end was originally of glass and the first floor frontage was taken up by five large windows, but this is no longer so. Between here and the *Boat* both narrow boats and barges are moored, Berkhamsted being the limit of the Grand Union as a proper barge canal. The third pub is the *Rising Sun*, dating at least from 1870, strategically placed beside a lock.

One of the pleasantest of the Grand Union pubs is the *Three Horseshoes* at Winkwell, beside a swing bridge. This is made up of three sixteenth-century cottages but is not recorded as a pub before

The *Crystal Palace*, Berkhamsted

1838. It is well kept with plenty of oak and a fine fireplace, the exterior being a deep peach-coloured wash. An ugly footbridge used to disfigure the scene, but this is now demolished. Nearby at Boxmoor is the *Fishery Inn*, one of the most photographed pubs on the Grand Union with its lounge window overhanging the water. This comprises a collection of buildings and goes back as a pub to 1839. The *Fishery* was a haven for the 'Idle Women', the volunteers who helped the national effort by working on the boats during the war and whose chronicler, Susan Woolfitt, described vividly their experiences in the book of that name. The weather was always fine when they tied up at the *Fishery*, but its chief merit was that it was

one of the only two pubs they found which provided baths .. 'even
if it did entail taking rags and Vim with you and half an hour's hard
work before you could decently leave the bathroom "as you would
wish to find it".'

There are several pubs along the southernmost part of the Grand
Union, including the *Batchworth Arms* by Batchworth lock, the
Fisheries by Copper Mill lock and the *Paddington Packet Boat* near
Cowley Peachey junction. At Bulls Bridge road, near the junction
with the Paddington arm, is another reminder of the original company—the *Grand Junction Arms*. Opposite a timber wharf which
still handles some traffic off the Thames and on the edge of an area
which has become in the last few years strongly reminiscent of old
Bengal, this pub has been altered more than once and is a far
remove from the little country canalside pub of the late nineteenth
century, depicted in a contemporary painting. A far remove too is
the almost deserted canal from the once busy waterway with boats
loading and unloading and twenty pairs filling the lay-by at Bulls
Bridge depot.

Northwards at Braunston the line divides by the *Rose & Castle*,
one of the best known of canalside pubs. It used to be a modest
Victorian house called the *New Castle*, but now you can take your
drink in the wardroom, admire the un-nautical wrought iron, and
stroll out on to the canal boatdeck to gaze on the craft moored below. An extension resembling a Mississippi steamer sails safely on
dry land above the murky water of the cut; it was the recipient of a
Civic Trust award a few years ago. Aesthetically the *Rose & Castle*
may be controversial; but it is hospitable to boat crews and if you
are heading for Birmingham along the line shared for part of the
way with the Oxford Canal it is nearly 10 miles before you reach
the next pub, the *Boat* at Birdingbury wharf.

The *Boat* is at the top of the Stockton locks, a pleasant old pub
where the boatmen could buy bread and other basic necessities as
well as beer. At the bottom of the flight is the *Blue Lias*, another
pub which evolved from a farmhouse. About three centuries old, it
has held a full licence for only about 10 years, but under its present
ex-Wing Commander landlord it has made up much leeway since.
It is a geological rather than a canal pub, Blue Lias being a purplish
clay found in the vicinity, and otherwise mostly in Devon. The

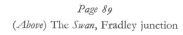

Page 89

(*Above*) The *Swan*, Fradley junction

(*Below*) The *Bird in Hand*, Kent Green, Macclesfield Canal

Page 90

(*Above*) The *Tontine Hotel*, Stourport

(*Below*) *The Packet*, Misterton, Chesterfield Canal

sign shows a prehistoric animal whose precise variety is a popular topic for discussion in the bar. The *Blue Lias* has a remarkable collection of photographs of airmen, aircraft and racing cars, reflecting the personal interests of its landlord.

Its nearest neighbour is the *Two Boats Inn* at Long Itchington, a white-painted brick building of about the same age as the canal. This is also a friendly pub, with its interior comparatively little altered. Facing the canal, it is more of a canalside pub than the *Blue Lias*; the two provide an intriguing contrast, each attractive in its own way.

From the *Two Boats* it is a long and thirsty road again; eleven locks to the summit, a dreary journey through the least fashionable part of Leamington Spa and around the outskirts of Warwick to the *Cape of Good Hope*. This whole area is called the Cape—it even has another pub called the *Governor's House*. The *Cape of Good Hope* originated with the cutting of the canal at the end of the eighteenth century, as a beerhouse with a smallholding; its name may simply derive from the fact that it was a long way from the centre of Warwick for the traveller on foot. It has two or three small cottages adjoining it and used to have stabling for seven horses and a smithy nearby. The pub has remained in the same family for generations, always closely connected with the life of the canal outside its front door. Intimately, one may say; the grandfather of Doris, the present landlady, was drowned in Cape lock, a few yards from the house. It is still—or was until recently—used by a working boatman doing it the hardest way of all, hauling a load of wood waste up Hatton flight by manpower alone. The interior of the pub is simple, with a good collection of 'hanging plates' on the walls.

At the top of Hatton, though not canalside, is the *New Inn*; then apart from the *Black Boy* south of Knowle there is nothing until Birmingham—and not very much there unless one leaves the water and ventures into the city. The *Longboat* at Farmer's bridge is worth a call, as one of the very few entirely new canalside pubs built in recent times. It is part of Birmingham Corporation's development of what used to be Cambrian wharf, and inside is like a miniature museum of canal relics. Faced with the necessity for reconstructing this area, the Corporation have gone to great trouble over scale and detail. The *Longboat* is very popular, and although devotees of

F

Victorian canal architecture may regret what has gone, the least they can do is to appreciate that with other local authorities this might simply have become another car park.

At Norton junction, east of Braunston, an arm of the Grand Union heads for Leicester. There is a cider house, the *Stag's Head*, close to the canal before the Watford flight of locks, but after that, as the Governor of North Carolina said to the Governor of South Carolina—or vice versa—'it's a long time between drinks'. There are plenty of bridges on the summit level, which winds vaguely through pleasant, undramatic countryside, and two tunnels, at Crick and Husbands Bosworth; but the beerhouses of the past have gone. A diversion on to the Welford arm leads to the *Wharf House Hotel* and the Market Harborough arm leads to the *Six Packs* (this referred to elsewhere). Half a mile along the latter arm is the *Black Horse* at Foxton. There is no substantiation for the story that Gordon Thomas, the engineer of the Foxton inclined plane, lived here while supervising its construction; he is more likely to have lodged more luxuriously in Market Harborough. The main line meanders on through Saddington tunnel now on the water of one of the longest named of the old canal companies, the Leicestershire & Northamptonshire Union. Saddington is reputedly haunted, but the farm at Kibworth which used to sell beer and where one could discuss the pros and cons of the ghost story sells beer no longer. At Kilby bridge you become aware of the approach of Leicester; a *Navigation Inn* at least as early as 1830 and possibly older than the canal, with one unspoiled room, faces the busy A50. There was a coal wharf here and a company house, lived in for years by George Foxton, surveyor to the company and a coal trader, who became company chairman in 1869. The only other pub before Leicester is the *County Arms* at Blaby, which so appalled Mr L. T. C. Rolt when he came across it on his classic voyage in *Cressy*, of which you can read in *Narrow Boat*, that no further comment is necessary.

North of Leicester on the Soar Navigation at Syston the wharf has been converted, almost inevitably, into a car park of quite remarkable starkness. The car park belongs to the *Hope & Anchor*, dating from the early nineteenth century. It may have been built as the house of the wharf owner. It is mentioned in the will of Sir Archdale Robert Palmer of Wanlip Hall in 1889 and later was owned by Everards Brewery of Leicester. When the establishment was sold in 1928, a coach house, skittle alley, pig sty, manure pit and stables went with it. The *Hope & Anchor* is a three-storey building, white painted and busy with callers from the main road, but its small bar rooms help to preserve a friendly atmosphere.

The old *Duke of York* at Mountsorrel, which dated from the 1790s and may have been a toll-collector's house, has recently been transmogrified into the *Waterside Inn*, and there are some people who may prefer it this way. The little *Navigation Inn* at Barrow-on-Soar has escaped this fate. This house was bought by the Leicester Navigation Company in 1861 for £200. The company owned the adjacent mill and some cottages and, with the decline in waterborne trade, wanted a profitable investment. They retained ownership until 1920, letting the property to a succession of tenants, and then sold it for £650. It is still a simple little house, with beer from the barrel, a working-man's pub of the old tradition.

There are two uncompromising canalside pubs in Loughborough, the *Boat* and the *Albion*, with their front doors opening on to the towpath. The *Boat* belonged to the Leicester Navigation Co in 1794, and passed through several hands, including those of a blacksmith, before it became brewery property in 1909. It once had its own brewhouse as well as piggeries and a skittle alley. From Loughborough it is about 9 miles of pleasant cruising to the junction with the Trent, with the *Plough* in the attractive village of Normanton for refreshment on the way.

8

CANALSIDE 2
The Oxford Canal

~~~~~~

It is difficult to imagine that most leisurely and amiable of waterways, the South Oxford Canal, as a busy commercial route. From
its winding course, with a lock here and there, one might think it
was designed to avoid the centres of population, not to serve them.
Begun by Brindley and finished after his death by Samuel Simcock
it was the archetypal contour canal. Several miles were lopped off
the North Oxford in later years when much of the line was
straightened by means of embankments and cuttings, but the
southern section remained unaltered, meeting the Cherwell now
and then as it wanders around the gentle hills.

Oxford in 1949 deposited Nuffield College and the adjacent car
park on the site of the canal basin and wharves, disposed of by the
canal company in 1937. It has been a prosperous undertaking in its
time, with tolls in the early nineteenth century reaching a high point
of £90,000 a year, and paying dividends of more than 30 per cent. A
photograph taken in the 1890s shows the busy Hayfield wharf of
Frank Restall, where three narrow boats have just unloaded a large

quantity of stone. Frank, his wife and foreman stand in the fore-ground; his leather aproned workmen stop pushing their assortment of wheelbarrows to gaze at the camera, as do six boatwomen in spotless white aprons, some wearing voluminous white mob-caps and all decorously posed. Indeed, the canal company was still viable financially up to the outbreak of World War II.

There seem to have been no public houses immediately adjoining the basin, but the *Queen's Arms* and the *Greyhound* were not far away. By the Cherwell, which enters Oxford parallel to the line of the canal, there is the reconstructed *Nag's Head*. Lower Fisher Row, a terrace of picturesque but doubtless insalubrious cottages where many boatmen lived, has been demolished, now, like Abel Beesley, university waterman, with his punt stacked high with bundles of reeds, a haunting memory in the whirling rush of traffic that monopolises this present abominable area. The canal can be found on the north side of Hythe bridge, a strip of dirty water bordering the bottom of the gardens of Worcester College. Past Isis lock and the Juxon Street wharf things improve as the canal heads out of Oxford for the countryside to the north.

There is a surprise north of Kidlington; three canalside pubs within a mile. The first is an old coaching inn, the *Wise Alderman*, which has stood fast for some 300 years while the road and then the railway in front of it have both been shifted up and down. It now stands below the level of the road, with the canal alongside it. When the railway opened it became called the *Railway Hotel*; its present name is a witty tribute from the brewers to the memory of a popular local figure, Mr Wise, a railway signalman who became an alderman and chairman of the bench. The sign bears his portrait. It is a long, low building, pleasant inside and out, and now draws some trade from pleasure boats. It was not a true canal pub, however, as was the *Jolly Boatman* at Thrupp, by the next bridge north. This has also undergone a change of name, being until recently called the *Britannia* and still familiarly known as the 'Brit'. The brewers wanted to rechristen it the *Jolly Bargeman*: at this heresy, for no bargemen ever navigated the Oxford nor any other canal where the locks were only 7ft wide, there was a chorus of protest led by Mrs Rose Beecham, the Grand Old Lady of the Oxford Canal, Mr Jack James, ex boat captain and guardian of canal lore, and the BWB

Museum. They corrected the error and checked the accuracy of the new sign. It had to be right; this was a favourite pub with the Oxford Canal boat people, many of whom held wedding parties here after a ceremony in Kidlington church. It is likely that the pub was built to serve the canal. It has been extended and modernised, but still remains very much part of the scene.

The canalside village of Thrupp had two more pubs, the *Boat* and the *Three Horseshoes*. The latter has gone, but the *Boat*, situated

The *Jolly Boatman*, Thrupp, Oxford Canal

behind the end of a row of cottages facing the canal, is there today, busy at times with waterborne customers as in the past. Although confined to one bank, Thrupp might serve as a model for the canalside settlement; all that it lacks now is the shop for the boat family's essentials. There is a lift bridge, a maintenance yard and a sharp right-angled bend whence for a space the canal occupies the bed of the Cherwell, the river having been diverted when the canal was made.

For several miles working northwards the canal passes through beautiful countryside, but with hardly a public house in sight. There is of course the *Rock of Gibraltar*, at Bletchington, where a new road bridge is replacing the narrow old Gibraltar bridge that added character but not safety to the crossing. The *Rock* and its grounds belonged to the canal company until 1932, when it was sold for £1,550. In 1947, when it was resold, the tenant was paying a rent of £52 a year—about the same amount a lock-keeper used to earn about 150 years before. There is no longer a *Three Pigeons* inn by Pigeon's lock, and it is about 11 miles before the next one, the *Great Western Arms* at Aynho wharf, a pleasant and friendly house between the wharf, now a hire-cruiser base, and the railway. With a road in front of it and Hook Norton beers no pub could be better fitted to serve all means of inland transport.

Both canal and railway amble on to Banbury, where the canal basin was filled in about 10 years ago for a bus station. It may be unfair to blame the local authority for failing to have the forethought to realise that this extensive basin could prove in future years a great asset to the town. As the only place of any size on the southern Oxford, Banbury is much visited by canal holidaymakers; private enterprise will reap the benefit of providing for their needs, while Banbury's buses have plenty of room to manoeuvre. One of the longest established boatyards still in business, Tooley's, is at Banbury, but it is now reduced to a repair yard and is possibly to disappear in a redevelopment plan. There is a description of the yard in *Narrow Boat*. The year in which Rolt cruised the canals was 1939; he mentions the *George and Dragon* at Fenny Compton, which then had no water supply and only a disused wharf as company. Now a large marina has been opened next to the pub. Rolt also spent an evening at the *Bull and Butcher* at Napton. He gives a wonderfully evocative description: narrow boats moored at the field's end, the one room with its paraffin lamp, the landlord pouring beer from a jug, two boat captains, each wearing a single gold ear-ring, playing darts while their wives talked quietly together. There is no *Bull and Butcher* at Napton now.

The village of Cropredy, 4 miles north of Banbury, is old and the canal's presence is only coincidental. It is the River Cherwell that is significant in Cropredy's history, recalled by the plaque on the bridge which reads: 'The site of the Battle of Cropredy Bridge in 1644. From Civil War deliver us.' Charles I had made Oxford his headquarters during the Civil War and at Cropredy his forces defeated an attempt by Cromwellian troops under Colonel Waller to cross the river in preparation for an assault on Oxford. In the fine old church of St Mary there are cannonballs and other relics of the battle.

Cropredy has no canalside pub, but the *Red Lion* is a short walk up the main street. It is a walk well worth taking. Temple Thurston, in his book *The 'Flower of Gloster'*, first published in 1911, devotes a chapter to the *Red Lion*. His boatman, Eynsham Harry, introduced him to the pub: 'This is Cropredy, sur—Cropredy Bridge. We'll just get through the lock and stop a bit. I always go here to the *Red Lion* for a drink.' On this authority, a sound one because Eynsham Harry was a boatman of long experience, the *Red Lion* counts as a canal pub. It is stone-built, probably sixteenth century, with a thatched roof. 'Where is the man who would not have stepped in ?' asked Temple Thurston. He and Harry played darts with two farm-hands; then he went across to the churchyard and thought how much he'd like to be a vicar in a country parish. Nearly 30 years later L. T. C. Rolt visited the *Red Lion*, finding it much as it was in Temple Thurston's time; both gentlemen commented favourably on the clear, cool beer, drawn straight from the wood in the cellar. It is a very pleasant pub still; indeed, with its church, the *Red Lion* and an excellent baker, and the canal and river together at the foot of the main street, Cropredy is a village of rare and intriguing charm.

The last pub on the southern Oxford is the *Napton Bridge Inn*, where A425 crosses the canal north-west of the village. It is an old house, perhaps as much as 400 years old, and an inn before the coming of the canal, being known then as the *New Inn*. It is on the summit level of the canal near to Napton junction, where the Oxford joins the Grand Union coming in from Birmingham and shares the same water until they part again at Braunston, the northern Oxford heading up to Hawkesbury and the Grand Union turning Londonwards beneath the windows of the *Rose and Castle*.

There is a long publess stretch northwards from Braunston until Newbold-on-Avon, on the north side of Rugby. Here is a tunnel about 250yd long constructed when many sections of the line of the Oxford were straightened in the 1820s. A portal of the original Newbold tunnel is in a field beside the graveyard of Newbold church and the winding course of the cut off loop can be traced here and there. Down a lane leading straight into the canal near the south end of the present tunnel are two pubs next to each other, the *Boat* and the *Barley Mow*. Study of the levels shows that this lane was not part of the original canal but was a very short arm or dock, with a wharf opposite the *Boat*. Research into the early history of the Oxford Canal may reveal facts about these two houses, but the *Boat* is claimed to have been a pub for 210 years which, if accurate, would make it earlier than the cutting of the canal.

On A4114, the Fosse Way, at Stretton, standing above both railway and canal each of which runs in a cutting below it, is the *Railway Inn*, the present building replacing one burnt down 100 years ago. When the stables on the canal bank were closed, the landlord of the *Railway* used to provide stabling for the boat horses at a charge of sixpence a night, enough to pay his rent. It took an average of four days for boats to reach London from here, yet coal deliveries by canal were often speedier than by rail because of the time lost when wagons stood motionless in sidings. Having for so long served both railway and canal, the *Railway Inn* now serves the road, encapsulating transport history, the pessimists might say. At Stretton Stop, below the pub, where tolls used to be collected, there is a hire-cruiser base; the canal narrowed at the Stop so that boats could not evade the attentions of the toll-collector.

The North Oxford Canal has lost most of its old pubs, but there are two left approaching the junction with the Coventry Canal at Hawkesbury. The first is at Tusses bridge: the *Elephant & Castle*. The bridge itself was rebuilt in the 1930s to replace a narrow hump-backed one. If you ask at the *Greyhound* at Hawkesbury whether you can walk to the *Elephant* along the towpath you may be greeted with roars of laughter and the story of the man who asked the same question one evening and was fished out of the canal the next day. Ten shillings was the reward for dragging the body out, and all who called in to see if they could recognise him looked with envy at his good pair of shoes. The *Elephant & Castle* used to be a farm and owned the land on which the power station now stands. It has plenty of stabling, in good preservation, used only recently to accommodate the motive power of a horse-drawn pleasure boat. The landlord, Mr Robert Sephton, belongs to a family which owned one of the longest-lived of the boat-building yards, just by the bridge, and still uses the yard's rubber stamp for clerical purposes.

Hawkesbury junction is 5 miles from the centre of Coventry and used to be one of the busiest points on the Midlands network. Here, at a lock with a fall of only 6in, the Oxford meets the Coventry Canal. Coventry basin is 5½ miles southwards; Fazeley junction, and the Birmingham & Fazeley Canal, 21½ miles north-west. Originally the Oxford and Coventry canals met nearly a mile towards Coventry, having run parallel for that distance owing to a failure to reach agreement over where and how they should join. The present junction dates from the 1830s.

The *Greyhound* at Sutton Stop, as the junction was known to boatmen after the name of a long-serving nineteenth-century tollkeeper there, used to be a signally popular pub in the days of commercial traffic. The building was originally the pay office of the Victoria Pit and provided stabling for the pit horses. When the junction was made the stabling was extended for the use of the canal horses and the office became a pub. The present kitchen and cellar were at one time part of the stables. One of the *Greyhound*'s two public rooms still remains much as it was a hundred years ago, with high-backed settles, tobacco-coloured walls and the old brick fireplace. There is a good collection of model boats and traditionally painted canal ware, much of it by the Ward family which boasted 22 children. The *Greyhound*'s old customers from the cut still crowd the boatmen's room, especially at Easter and Christmas Eve. It used to be a great place for singing and dancing to the sound of the accordion. The grey, spartan exterior of the *Greyhound* belies the friendliness within.

Hawkesbury junction is well worth examining in some detail. Opposite the pub a handsome cast-iron bridge, made in the Britannia Foundry, Derby, in 1837, carries the towpath across to the Coventry arm. Nearby, though in sorry condition, is the old pumping house erected in 1821. The pumping engine, a Newcomen type which used to be nicknamed 'Lady Godiva', was removed by the Newcomen Society in 1963 and is now housed in the museum at Dartmouth, where Newcomen was born. It ceased working at Hawkesbury in 1913.

There are always some boats moored at the entrance to the

Coventry arm, and amongst them you may see Mr and Mrs Skinner's narrow boat *Friendship*, the last of the horse-drawn boats to trade on the Oxford Canal. The canal is navigable into Coventry and there are ambitious plans for the reconstruction of the basin. The energetic Coventry Canal Society is promoting schemes for the improvement of the waterway and its immediate surroundings. Among its proposals, however, it calls for a renovated public house at the junction. At the moment, road access to the *Greyhound* is by means of a pot-holed track that leads from the main road beneath a disused wooden railway bridge and debouches the surprised traveller into what is architecturally still a nineteenth-century canal-side settlement, although there is no longer a Salvation Army chapel and the shops have closed. Behind the *Greyhound* are the remains of the old pit workings, and looming over all are the cooling towers of Longford Power Station. But the junction is not just a museum piece; the pleasure cruisers have brought back life and colour to the waterway and the interior of the *Greyhound* exudes the life and colour of the past. It does not need the hand of the modern architect to 'improve' it.

9

CANALSIDE 3
Great National Undertakings

〜〜〜〜〜〜〜〜〜〜〜〜〜〜〜〜〜〜〜〜〜〜〜〜〜〜〜〜〜〜

A waterways map of England shows two roughly parallel lines over the north-west: the main line of the Shropshire Union, and the Trent & Mersey Canal until it swings away through Fradley junction. They provide some contrasts in engineering, with Telford's deep cuttings and high embankments on the Shropshire Union (originally the Birmingham & Liverpool Junction Canal) solving problems of dealing with contours in a different way from that adopted by Brindley on the Trent & Mersey some 60 years earlier. Both canals are popular cruising waterways and both have retained some of the old pubs which used to provide the working boatman with refreshment, groceries, appropriate items of chandlery, stabling for his horse, and sometimes lodging for the night.

There is no pub today at Autherley junction, where the Shropshire Union and Staffordshire & Worcestershire canals meet, though one feels that with the amount of pleasure traffic at this point one might now be in demand. The *Bridge*, by the bridge at Brewood, used to be a one-room inn and the present Smoke Room has been made out of the old stables. A mock Tudor frontage tells of nothing but the taste of its designer; the older, mellower construction may be seen at the rear of the building. This pub faces the road, while the *Hartley Arms* at Wheaton Aston, the next village north, faces the canal. This old pub has recently been extended and modernised but is externally still appropriate in its setting.

The village of Gnosall has two canalside pubs. The *Boat* is the older; it was a cottage—or perhaps two cottages—when the canal was cut, and was turned into a pub to serve the new trade. There was stabling for eleven horses and moorings for three pairs of

The *Star*, Stone, Trent & Mersey Canal

narrow boats, further moorings being available on the other side of the adjacent bridge. The interior of the pub is now one large public room of curious shape with a bay window overlooking the water. The council yard on the opposite side of the road was once a wharf and in its time has been a timber yard where mangles were made, a brickworks and a milk and cheese depot. The landlord being a local councillor, conversation in the *Boat* may be weightier than in other inns. Gnosall's other pub, the *Navigation*, dates from about 1860 and was probably built specifically for canal custom. Being on the towpath side it had no stabling of its own. Beer was delivered from fly-boats—the equivalent of the express goods train—through a door into the basement from the towpath. Inside, navigation has been interpreted in a different way, with the accent on the naval style of the days of Nelson.

At Norbury, where the sadly disused Newport arm that once connected with the waterway network of East Shropshire was legally abandoned in 1944, the *Junction Inn* flourishes opposite an equally flourishing boatyard. It was built about the same time as the canal but has been extensively modernised since the last war. Being patronised by some who learn their living from the canal helps it to retain a trace of an old flavour, and Tony Lewery's colourful murals do their best to keep some picture of the past before us. There is more flavour, however, to the *Anchor* at High Offley—that is, if you can ever find it open. This isolated house was kept by the same landlady for nearly 70 years, for the last 40 on her own after her husband died. The *Anchor* was built about 1830, and preserves the same benches and tables in the bar that it has always had. The pub was known as 'Sebastopol' to the owners, while the boatmen called it the 'New House'. When Mrs Pascall and her husband took over early this century the beer was delivered by horse and cart from Wellington. Her husband ran the local milk boat. The *Anchor* was busy then, with boatmen and their families singing and sometimes dancing; they ran a football team and had a supper every Saturday night. In the mornings the boatmen would call in for a drink about six o'clock, before moving on. Mrs Pascall made her own butter and cheese and put on wellington boots to fetch the beer up from the cellar. After 1945, when the working boats became fewer and fewer, trade almost disappeared but, in the words of the present landlord, Mrs Pascall's grandson, 'we did not let the inn die'.

The *Anchor* is a plain-looking house. It has two public rooms, but only one of them was regularly used, and that not 'the best'. There was no proper road access until about 15 years ago. The stables, for six or eight horses, are still there. Trade is coming back to the *Anchor* now, from the crews of pleasure boats and from people who like things as they were. When the living accommodation is improved the pub will be open every day again; fortunately the landlord intends to maintain the pub's tradition and to continue serving the beer directly from the cellar. Surely he deserves every support.

A mile north-west from High Offley the little *Wharf Inn* crouches beneath the aqueduct at Shebdon, by the beginning of the massive Shebdon embankment. It is about 400 years old and was an estate house. Its licence made it close half an hour earlier than other pubs in the vicinity so that the drunken peasantry would be out of the way when the gentry arrived home. As it was accessible from the canal above it became popular with boatmen and used to provide stabling. Alterations within have not been drastic; it has three small rooms instead of one large one, while the meat hooks on the ceiling disclose that the public bar was once the kitchen. 'Our Lily' remembers the boatmen dancing at Christmas, and it is still possible to visualise the scene. Very different is this *Wharf* from the next—the *Wharf Tavern* at Goldstone wharf, Cheswardine. Here is an attractive old building, energetically catering for trade from both road and canal. But somehow one cannot imagine a boatman's big boots on that carpet.

The canal avoids most of Market Drayton—there would not be room for it anyway among the traffic. The large and solid-looking *Talbot* provides the last refreshment for about 6 miles. It used to keep a special room for the noisy boatmen. Then comes the *Bridge Inn* at Audlem. The part of the building nearest the canal was an old beerhouse, contemporary with the canal, and had a stable door opening on to the towpath. At the back were stabling for eleven horses and a wharf where stone and meal were the main cargoes loaded. If you are on a boat travelling north the *Bridge* is certainly worth a stop, especially as it is the last pub for 10 miles. Nantwich junction—the junction between Telford's line and the old Chester Canal—is now publess; so is Hurleston junction, where the Llangollen Canal heads off to the west. Barbridge junction compensates to some extent with two pubs. The *King's Arms*, a small house in the village, backs on to the canal. It is a plain brick-built pub with an interior that cannot have been greatly altered since it was first opened. There was stabling for four horses. In the days of commercial traffic on the canals the main pub here would have been the predecessor of the new *Jolly Tar*, reputedly a great place for fights amongst boatmen, exactly opposite the junction with the Middlewich branch that links the Shropshire Union to the Trent & Mersey. At the wharf here 60lb cheeses were loaded for Manchester every Friday evening in years past—Cheshire cheese actually came from Cheshire, difficult to realise in this age of prepackaged slices in the supermarket. A warehouse used to span the canal in the past; the present is imposed by a progressive marina on the Middlewich arm, so progressive that it displays its name prominently and deplorably on the well-proportioned canal bridge.

The next true canalside pub is the isolated *Royal Oak* at Tiverton, although the *Davenport Arms* at Calveley may qualify as it was quite close to the wharf. The *Royal Oak* is beside Bates Mill bridge, within sight of Beeston castle. As a building it predates the canal; it was a cottage that became used as the office for a coal wharf when trading got under way. Later it became an inn and has been extended recently without spoiling the appearance of the building. It is nicknamed the 'Shady Oak'; there used to be one beside it, one of the several hundred in which King Charles is supposed to have hidden—if only half the stories are true he must have spent more time up aloft than on the ground. This is a friendly pub with good moorings. It is now not very far to Chester; at Christleton, where the 1950 Grand National winner Russian Hero was trained, *Ye Old Trooper* (a pity about the 'ye' which can best be described as an Old English illiteracy) with its heavy frontage seems as if it is trying to push the humbler rear of its buildings into the canal itself. Then comes Chester, entered past the *Lock Vaults*, of which the most attractive feature is its sign showing the lock with the pub in the background, with its sign . . . etc. The principal wharf of the Chester Canal Company was at Cow Lane, now called Frodsham Street although the canal bridge is known still as Cow Lane bridge. By the wharf were canal offices and a warehouse and there was another warehouse with a yard belonging to the company on the opposite side of the street. On the street corner facing the site of the wharf is a pub bearing the date 1771, the *Oddfellows' Arms*. As it is probable that a passenger service in the early years of the canal operated from here it is also probable that the *Oddfellows'* served the purpose later fulfilled by the railway hotel. It is not likely that it was built by the company as the Act for the canal was not passed until 1772, work being started the same year. At the top of Northgate locks nearby, a plaque commemorates the 200th anniversary of the canal, if local vandals have not already defaced it entirely.

Page 107

(*Above*) The *Lowther Hotel*, Goole, in the 1920s

(*Below*) 'Charlotte Dundas' outside the *Barge Inn*, Honey Street, Kennet & Avon Canal

Page 108

(*Above*) The *Royal Oak*, Pencelli, Brecon & Abergavenny Canal

(*Below*) The *Bridge Inn*, Offenham, River Avon

It is not possible to say that the pubs alongside any one canal are 'typical' of that waterway; they have been subject to too many changes and differing pressures of demand for that. A look at the Trent & Mersey pubs reveals the present-day variety far more than any particular similarities between them. In some the links with the past are very tenuous indeed, if not invisible. At Preston Brook (strictly on the Bridgewater Canal, in the last few yards before it joins the Trent & Mersey at the tunnel), the *Red Lion* used to have stabling for about a hundred horses, which means that it must have been one of the liveliest pubs on the whole system. The boatmen's room here was known as the Jailhouse, for which there may have been any number of good reasons. Above Preston Brook, at Dutton, is a pub, the *Talbot Arms*, which appears to have no connection with the canal at all. It faces a busy main road and there is no water visible. In fact, the water is underneath—in the tunnel—and by the side of the pub was the boat road which linked the two portals. The *Talbot*, which before modernisation was a grim-visaged brick building, was known as the 'Tunnel Top' and served the boatmen who led their horses from one portal to the other while the boat was legged through below.

Neither of the above houses makes much of an architectural contribution to their locality, unlike the *Old Broken Cross* on the outskirts of Northwich, a handsome, white-painted brick house looking very much at ease in its surroundings. Only the ugly rebuilt canal bridge disturbs the harmony of the scene. The pub has several interesting outbuildings and there is a smithy over the road. In different ways some of the Middlewich pubs are also appropriate to the canalside. By the junction with the branch of the Shropshire Union the *King's Lock* dominates the lock of the same name. A split-level building, the lowest of the three storeys at the rear was once composed of stabling. The big lock in Middlewich is the first of the wide locks on this waterway coming up from the south. The pub by it is likewise *The Big Lock*, tucked into a corner by a mill and facing a lock cottage across the canal. The elaborate decorative stonework on the building indicates the architect's refusal to be quelled by the industrial setting. There are two ground floor levels to the pub, one for the street entrance and one for the canal, and a range of stabling attached, now looking forlorn.

G

Middlewich also has a *Cheshire Cheese*, backing on to the canal.
Then comes a succession of animals: a *Cheshire Cat* at Wheelock, a
Romping Donkey at Hassall Green, a seventeenth-century village
pub which had the canal cut alongside the rear of its premises and
provided stabling for boatmen's horses, and a *Red Bull* at Kids-
grove by the Red Bull locks. Amidst this miniature zoo is the
Broughton Arms at Rode Heath. This dates from about 1864; at
least, that is when the nearby row of cottages called Canal Terrace
was built. The pub may possibly be older. It contains a well-
preserved example of a canal horse harness, with colourfully painted
wooden bobbles. The *Broughton Arms* had stabling for seven; the
wooden fitments are still in position, and a working boatman from
the past could tie up, give his horse a drink from the trough in the
yard, stable him, use the boatman's lavatory—but he would find
the interior of the pub altered, and pleasantly so. Lily of the *Wharf
Inn* at Shebdon on the Shropshire Union stayed here during the
war and remembers being awakened at night by the horses stomp-
ing in the stables below her window. She also recalls the boat-
women in their blue and white striped skirts, white aprons and
clogs celebrating here at holiday time.

The junction with the Macclesfield Canal has two pubs opposite
each other, the *Blue Bell* and the *Canal Tavern*, near the entrance to
the long, dirty and scalp-endangering Harecastle tunnel, one of
Thomas Telford's engineering triumphs—as the adjacent disused
tunnel was one of Brindley's—but now a source of concern to
BWB on account of roof falls and subsidence. South of the tunnel
is the rusty-coloured water and industrial excitement of Stoke-on-
Trent, with the contrast of great steelworks and derelict pottery
bottle-kilns. The nearest pub to the tunnel is the *Duke of Bridgewater* at Longport. This eighteenth-century house was once the
home of a herbalist and pharmacist; it was licensed in 1834 and has
been recently renovated and extended. The extension overlooks the
canal and has been decorated with the canal very much in mind
with butty boat stern posts and tillers and roses on the legs of the
stools. It contrasts with another large pub, the *Bridge Inn* at
Etruria, where the factory of Josiah Wedgwood, the great cham-
pion of canals, once stood.

South of Stoke after a few miles the Trent & Mersey becomes a quiet rural waterway with few pubs. There is some activity and a monstrous gasholder at Stone; there is also the *Star Inn*, perhaps the oldest alongside this canal. It is claimed to date from the fourteenth century, and may well do so. The *Star* is an intriguing building with all its many small rooms on different levels; you go up and down stairs while still remaining on the same floor. It stands beside a lock and naturally used to provide stabling, now removed in the interests of a large car park.

Industry returns to the canal between Rugeley and Armitage.

The *Ash Tree*, Rugeley, Trent & Mersey Canal

Midway between them is the *Ash Tree*, a farmhouse built about the same time as the waterway was opened. The present bar used to be the farm kitchen, from where beer was sold to passing boatmen. There was a small basin on the site of the car park where coal used to be loaded, and cheese voyaged from here during the last war. The *Ash Tree*, run by two sisters, is an exceptionally well kept house

which sets out to cater for boat crews of today in an equally exceptional way. In this it is paralleled by the well-known *Swan* at
Fradley junction, where the Coventry Canal meets the Trent &
Mersey at its southernmost point. The Trent & Mersey was opened
throughout in 1777, and the *Swan*, with the group of canalside
buildings including a warehouse and a one-time trading post of
which it forms a part, dates from about this time. The junction,
however, was not made until 1790, as the Coventry Canal com-
mittee had for many years previous been directing their efforts
elsewhere, mainly influenced by the colliery owners among their
members who foresaw easing the path for their competitors if this
route were completed. Under pressure from other canal companies
and with a new view of the prospects as they saw how trade was
building up, the Coventry eventually completed their line and
Fradley junction became a busy little place. As indeed, after an
interval of some years quietude, it is again, but busy now with
pleasure cruisers. Fradley is remote from the through traffic of the
roads, the only access for vehicles being along the towpath which
has been sufficiently widened and surfaced as far as the group of
buildings which includes the *Swan*.

Up to 22 horses could be stabled at the *Swan*; some of the stables
still retain the troughs and wooden fitments. The house has an
interesting brick-vaulted cellar bar, with three bays. It is below the
level of the canal, and the overflow water from the locks runs along
a conduit beneath the floor. This bar, so far from the sea, is said to
have been a haunt of smugglers; in this case, the boatmen who
used to sell brandy obtained illicitly in the docks in London. With
a fitting, if ironical, sense of history, the present landlord has as
his own boat a converted Thames police launch, which is moored
opposite the pub.

The canalside buildings at Fradley junction, of which the
white-painted *Swan* is the central feature, form an attractively
harmonious architectural composition, more mellow, less stark
than the comparable group at Hawkesbury. The *Swan* is a friendly
pub and has attracted several writers who have published accounts
of their canal journeys. Here L. T. C. Rolt enjoyed a glass of beer
while his wife bought fruit from the old toll office opposite. Fred
Doerflinger described the *Swan* as 'a gem', and John Liley, without

apparently even calling at the pub, fell in the canal outside it twice. It has been modernised in recent years, but with its cellar bar, stables and framed historical maps and documents on its walls still retains many of its links with the past.

About 25 miles from Fradley the Trent & Mersey Canal ends, joining the rivers Trent and Derwent at Shardlow. Despite the busy A6, the canal is the focal point of Shardlow, with its handsome warehouses, Stevens' corn mills, Dobson's boatyard and the canal-side pubs. The *Navigation* does face the main road, but both the *Malt Shovel* and the *New Inn* are canal-oriented. The *Malt Shovel* was built in 1799 as the house for the manager of the adjacent maltings. When it became a licensed house the name *Malt Shovel* was transferred to it as being more appropriate from another pub in the village, which in turn was renamed *Canal Tavern*, though this has now gone. It is quite a complicated little building; the cellars stretch under the old malthouse, which is now living accommodation for the landlord, and the pub itself has been remodelled inside. During these building operations there were some strange happenings: a bricked-up doorway was opened overnight and the bricks piled up over the floor; the builder's apprentice claimed to have been pushed down a flight of stairs when there was nobody else in the house; and the builder himself, not a specially impressionable man, staggered white-faced into the bar after having undergone the same experience. Responsibility for these occurrences was ascribed to Humphrey, the ghost of a tramp allegedly drowned in a vat by the foreman of the maltings in the early days. The first owner of the maltings was a Mr Humphrey, which explains where the name came from; but there are no other explanations. Since the building alterations were completed, however, Humphrey has not manifested himself again. A more tangible relic of the past is a mooring chain dating from the very early nineteenth century, found when the road, which is also the towpath, was dug up for the insertion of piping and showing by its position that the canal used to be about 5ft wider than it is today.

The *Malt Shovel* is complemented by the *New Inn*, a few yards away on the same side of the canal. This was formed in the early nineteenth century from a terrace of four canal cottages and like its neighbour must be as busy now as it was in the days of Shardlow's canal-borne prosperity. But the old cottages on the far side of the canal from the *New Inn* are due for demolition, as is the warehouse opposite the *Malt Shovel*. One can only hope that Shardlow will be as fortunate in the architecture of the replacements for these buildings as it was when it first came into being as a trans-shipment port at the terminus of the Trent & Mersey Canal.

10

CANALSIDE 4
Northwards

The Shropshire Union and the Trent & Mersey are both predominantly rural in character and are popular with holidaymakers in the summer. The Bridgewater Canal, which is owned by the Manchester Ship Canal Company and not by the British Waterways Board, is less of a pleasure waterway; the boats using it are more likely to be owned by those living in the area than hired by people from other parts. Generally, therefore, the public houses have not set out to cater for the holiday trade and, whatever their past, seem today to be little affected by the canal no matter how close to their walls it runs. Without the canal, of course, some of the pubs would never have been built at all. There are two of this kind facing each other in Broad Heath, Altrincham, separated by Navigation Road. One is the *Old Packet Boat*, whence in the 1830s and 40s packet-boats used to run to Manchester and Runcorn, the journeys taking two to five hours respectively. The fare to Manchester was 9d in the 'front room' and 6d in the 'back room'. Until quite recently coal was off-loaded here for a printing works nearby. The *Navigation Inn*

was built for the canal in 1780; the present dreary building, erected
in 1937, incorporates the brown-painted portico of the original.
The grim-looking *Bridge* at Sale is also clearly a canal-purpose pub.

One of the major works on the canal is the embankment at
Bollington, with an aqueduct over the River Bollin. A breach in
this embankment recently caused the closure of the canal for
several months. Near the western end of the embankment is the
Swan with Two Nicks—the correct version of this name, the two
nicks in a swan's bill being the mark of ownership of the Vintners'
Company. This dates from about 1700, a village pub close to the
river and handy for agricultural labourers and workers at the mill.
It became used by Bridgewater boatmen, there being nowhere
along the top of the embankment to stop for a drink, and stabling
was put up at the rear. A little ivy-covered plain place in the 1880s,
it has now adopted a wrought-iron elegance inside and become
popular with those escaping for a while from the urban conglomeration to the east.

The breach in the embankment resulted in the Inland Waterways
Association holding its National Rally of Boats at Lymm in 1972,
the profits from which were put towards the cost of the repair work.
Brindley cut his canal right through the village of Lymm, containing it in an aqueduct that altered the old road pattern almost beyond
recognition. Lymm's real canal pub, the *Bridgewater Arms*, presumably the 'neat and clean' public house where passengers could
refresh themselves when the packet-boats used to halt for 15min,
c 1800, has been demolished. The *Bull's Head*, however, still
flourishes. This was about a hundred years old when the canal
arrived and you can see from the levels how the road in front of it
was raised to make the hump-backed bridge. For many years the
Bull's Head was a lodging house for boatmen, who stabled their
horses at the rear. The sandstone cellars beneath the pub were
carved out of the rock. Salt was carried from Lymm in the nineteenth century, but the characteristic local industry was fustian-
cutting—fustian being a thick twill cloth with a short nap, made
from cotton, hard-wearing and usually dyed a dark colour, fit for
the working classes rather than for the gentry. Boats took the fustian
to Manchester and Runcorn and thence to all parts of the kingdom.
Opposite the *Bull's Head* is another pleasant pub, the *Golden Fleece*,

where a fustian-cutting shop was knocked down when the present car park was made. This demolition revealed a length of the original canal retaining wall, with deeply incised masons' marks on each of the large blocks of stone. 'W' was responsible for at least 14 of the stones now visible. At the back of the *Golden Fleece* the canal is carried by an aqueduct over a road and the Bradley Brook.

The northern arm of the Bridgewater Canal connects with the Leeds & Liverpool at Leigh, the Bridgewater having crossed the

The *Anchor*, Salterforth, Leeds & Liverpool Canal

Ship Canal by the famous Barton swing aqueduct. The Leeds & Liverpool is the only one of the three trans-Pennine water routes still to be navigable; both the Huddersfield Narrow and the Rochdale—apart from a short stretch in Manchester—being abandoned and serving as water channels only. 127 miles long, with 16 miles of branches the Leeds & Liverpool is a waterway of the utmost variety and fascination. It developed its own peculiar type of boat, the short boat, its own technical vocabulary and, here and there, its own lock gear. It also has, near the border between Yorkshire and Lancashire at Salterforth, its own peculiar pub. The *Anchor* is really two pubs, one on top of the other. Here for over a hundred years before the cutting of the canal stood a small, two-storey roadside inn. When the canal arrived alongside the building, the road had to be raised for a bridge to be constructed. This left the bedrooms of the *Anchor* level with the road. Another storey was built on top and the bedrooms became the public rooms, now frequented by boatmen as well as coach travellers. The old ground floor rooms became the cellars, and in one of them stalactites began to form, the longest approaching 3ft. From the floor, stalagmites are beginning to arise to meet them. It is not what one expects to find next to a canal, although stalactites are in evidence in several tunnels. Somehow the Leeds & Liverpool is seeping into the *Anchor*'s cellar, but it is confined to the limestone and does not get into the beer.

There are few pubs on this superb Pennine section of the canal. Through traffic fell away long before commercial carrying diminished at each end, hence there are plenty of pubs surviving near Leeds and westwards from Wigan. The *Rodley Barge* at Farley was a popular mooring in commercial days when it was known as the *Three Horseshoes*; inside it preserves a boat stove and other relics of the past. There were stables on the other side of the road. The *Fishermans* at Bingley was, and likewise is, also popular; but if you were heading west and there was no room to tie up at the *Barge* it meant a lot of effort working up the Bingley Five and Three before you could relax at the *Fishermans*. There was never a pub at Saltaire, the next township, as Sir Titus Salt, who built this model town in the mid-nineteenth century, would not permit one. The brick-built, solid-looking *Marquis of Granby* faces the water at Stockbridge, one of the very few waterside pubs named after this nobleman who is remembered so often in this sphere.

Both Silsden and Skipton have well-proportioned canalside buildings, old warehouses converted now to other uses and, at Skipton, mills still in operation. The first stretch of the canal to open to boats was that between Bingley and Skipton, in 1773. Close to the canal basin is the *Rose & Crown* and a short distance away is the *Royal Shepherd*, at the end of a terrace of houses over-looking the beginning of the short Springs branch. These were also popular houses with the boatmen. The Springs branch, also and more grandly known as Lord Thanet's Canal, was made in the early days of the canal to connect limestone quarries behind Skipton

Castle with the main line. The branch is less than half a mile long and only a short length is now navigable—and you will probably have to come out in reverse. Along the towpath is Leatt's mill, an old watermill converted to an informal museum of what might be called agricultural archaeology; two working waterwheels operate a host of devices for doing every imaginable thing to grain and other agricultural produce. Opposite the mill there is a small pub tucked in between larger buildings and the canal—the *New Ship*. This was once part of a lodge of Skipton Castle, which rises behind it, the branch using part of the moat for its course. The *New Ship* is very small and preserves a decent Victorian air.

Two of the next three pubs are called the *Anchor*. Most easterly is the *Anchor* at Gargrave, by the wharf where lead and stone used to be loaded. A farmhouse first, then a small beerhouse with acetylene lamps, the *Anchor* is now a large modernised house providing all facilities; fortunately the result is happier than in many other instances. The pub provides moorings, but it is worth having a look at the level of the pound above before tying up as this is a notorious spot for finding oneself stuck in the mud with only a few inches of water. The River Aire bubbles through Gargrave, a pleasant little village. Up eight more locks and you are near the summit of the canal, high in the Pennines with magnificent open countryside through which the canal twists and winds as if to ensure that you can see everything for as long as possible. But what it must have been like in a cold winter in the days of the horse-drawn boats is unimaginable.

By the Double Bridge, where a new arch was built on top of an older one when the road level was raised, there is a late seventeenth-century inn, another which developed out of a farmhouse, the *Cross Keys*. It faces the road, in a small cluster of mellow old buildings, with its garden sloping down to the canal. The first known licensee of the *Cross Keys* also acted as a moneylender. The towpath here forms part of the Pennine Way. In the 9 miles between Gargrave and Salterforth the *Cross Keys* seems to have always been the only pub, making this a thirsty road for boatmen as well as an exposed one in harsh weather. The Greenberfield locks take the canal up to the summit level where the *Anchor* at Salterforth, already mentioned, is the only pub. The *Hole in the Wall* at Foulridge, near the

entrance to the tunnel, is up in the village. You will have to go
there if you want verification of the story of 'Buttercup', the cow
who fell into the canal and swam through the tunnel from the far
end, being revived with brandy to enjoy subsequent fame.

Westward to Wigan, in the vicinity of which there is a large
number of canalside pubs as if to compensate for the scarcity earlier.
For the most part they are straightforward canalside houses with no
written history. One of them, however, the *Seven Stars* near the
bridge of the same name in Wigan, emerged briefly into the lime-
light in 1775, before the canal's construction. The landlord and his
wife had gone out, leaving the pub in the charge of two maidserv-
ants and the ostler. A soldier called, claiming lodging; he was
given supper and then went to bed. The girls also retired but were
soon disturbed by noises as of someone breaking in. Suspecting the
soldier's integrity they went to his room but were 'agreeably disappointed' to find him asleep. They woke him, telling him they
suspected burglars. He arose and dressed; then, in the words of the
reporter of the *Cumberland Pacquet*,

> having charged his musket and pointed his bayonet, he ordered
> one of them to follow him downstairs, holding the candle over his
> shoulder. Just as they came to the head of the stairs, they heard
> some person sharpening a knife on one of the steps, and about the
> middle of the stairs they met the Ostler coming up with a large
> case-knife in his hand; he attempted to strike the soldier with it,
> who in the scuffle ran him through the body and he fell dead on the
> spot. The Soldier then ran into the kitchen where he found two
> other men, unarmed; they attempted to escape, but he declared if
> they persisted in it he would run one of them through the body and
> shoot the other. He then ordered the girls to run out and alarm the
> neighbourhood, which they did; the two surviving villains were
> next morning carried before the Magistrate, who committed them
> to Lancaster gaol . . .

The grateful landlord of the *Seven Stars* rewarded the soldier with
20 guineas.

Because of the number of pubs on this length of the Leeds &
Liverpool—more still if one includes the Rufford and Leigh
branches—it is difficult to avoid merely giving a list. Among the
others there are two near the top of the flight of 21 locks at Wigan:

two *Ships*, one at Burscough and one with a boatyard at Haskayne: the *Ring O'Bells*, west of Parbold, built in 1738, which became a stopping place on the Leeds to Wigan packet boat run and now has a good restaurant: the *Scarisbrick Arms*, nearly as old: and, very much older, the *Scotch Piper* at Lydiate, a short distance from Lollies bridge. This pub dates from 1320. Until about 1715 it was called the *Royal Oak*; legend has it that it was renamed after a piper who was wounded in battle in the '15 uprising. The daughter of the house rescued and hid him, tended his wounds and later became his wife. The inn deserves this romantic reputation; it was built around a tree, some of which can still be seen, and is a small house of much fascination and character.

11

CANALSIDE 5
Here and there

~~~~~~

Shropshire Union, Trent & Mersey, Leeds & Liverpool, Oxford—
and there are plenty of other Great National Undertakings with
public houses covering a similar range to those we have already
looked at. There are few, however, which connect you so strongly
to past canal history as the *Hopwood House*, on the Worcester &
Birmingham Canal. It is near the southern portal of West Hill
tunnel, by far the longest of the four tunnels on this heavily locked
waterway (58 locks in 30 miles). West (or Wast) Hill tunnel is
2,726yd long, exceeded only by Dudley, Blisworth, Netherton and
Harecastle of the tunnels still navigable—and Dudley only counts
under special limiting conditions. *Hopwood House* used to provide
sleeping quarters for the leggers who used to work boats through
West Hill. No luxury for them; they slept on the wide wooden
benches lining the room nearest to the road. The benches are
slightly hollowed in the centre to lessen the chances of their falling
off. The pub itself is a four-storey red-brick building facing the
canal and had plenty of stabling, some of which survives. In the

cellar there was a bakehouse. Not only did leggers sleep in the *Hopwood House*; on the top storey are six small bedrooms used by boatmen years ago. The pub was built about 1830, 15 years or so after the canal was opened throughout and when it was a busy and prosperous concern.

The Worcester & Birmingham is best known for the longest flight of locks on the system—the thirty locks of the Tardebigge flight, beating Caen Hill at Devizes by one. As if to make sure of the record, there are a further six locks in the Stoke flight, just below the bottom of Tardebigge. At the top there is a boatyard and a tunnel, but no pub; thirsty lock-wheelers have to go on to the *Crown* on the outskirts of Alvechurch for their merited refreshment. Fortunately, the *Crown* is worth waiting for; it is an old country pub, older than the canal. If you are in the private bar you are in what used to be the stables with an old hayloft above your head. Half way up, or down, the flight there used to be a convenient pub, called, reasonably enough, *Half Way House*, but it is now privately owned. At the bottom of the flight, however, something unusual has happened: the *Queen's Head* has reopened as a fully licensed house after 60 years when it was no more than an off licence and shop. Although the falling off of commercial boat traffic was the main reason for the closure, it was not the only one; the last landlord used to take delivery of about three barrels of beer a week, but drank most of it himself.

The Tardebigge locks look fiercer on the map than they are in reality. They are comparatively easy to work and have not detracted from this canal's popularity with present-day boat crews. Stoke wharf, by the bottom lock in the Stoke flight below Tardebigge, also adds to the canal's attractiveness with a harmonious group of brick buildings including a warehouse and, at a short remove from the canal, the *Navigation Inn*. South of here there are three more pubs close to the canal, the appropriately named *Boat and Railway* being one of them. Probably better known is the *Eagle and Sun* at Hanbury wharf, by a bridge where the Roman road, Salt Way, crosses the canal and close to the point where the disused Droitwich Junction Canal meets the Worcester & Birmingham. The Droitwich Junction, a narrow waterway connecting with the wide Droitwich Canal, which in turn connected with the Severn, was

abandoned in 1939. But there are moves in hand now to reopen
these waterways, thus restoring another valuable link to the system.
When the work is completed there will again be three exits to the
canal system from the Severn within a distance of about 12 miles: at
Worcester, Hawford (for Droitwich) and Stourport.

In the 48 miles of the Staffordshire & Worcestershire Canal from
Stourport to its junction with the Trent & Mersey at Great Hay-
wood there are several pleasant pubs. About 11 firms now hire
craft on this canal, and there are several boat-building and repair
yards, which gives some indication of its popularity. One of the
pubs is the attractive *Lock Inn* at Wolverley. This building was once
a pair of sixteenth-century cottages, which probably belonged to
nearby Wolverley Court. The cottages were knocked into one and
converted into a pub about the time of the cutting of the canal in the
late 1760s. A brewhouse was added; this has now been incorporated
in the building itself. Being by a main route, once a drovers' road,
from the Black Country to Wales, the *Lock* has always been busy
with road traffic as well as serving the canal. A previous landlord,
Harry Davies, held the licence for 55 years. It is said that it suited
both him and the boatmen for payment for beer to be made with
coal, or whatever negotiable cargo happened to be on board at the
time. His customers found this so convenient that many of them
ended up overnight on the kitchen floor, their pockets no lighter
than when they started drinking but otherwise rather the worse for
wear. The present licensee has a well-known collection of harness
and horse brasses. During recent alterations a reminiscence of a
pub which closed in 1849 was found; a pewter tankard engraved
with the name of J. Gardner, of the *Junction Inn*, Kidderminster.

Other pubs still open along this canal include the *Navigation* at
Greensforge, also a lockside house, and the *Round Oak* at Roundel
bridge. Presumably it is drinkers from this latter inn who appear in
large numbers at the Bratch locks, half a mile to the north, whenever a pleasure boat crew are about to tackle them for the first time.
But disaster seldom occurs, probably because there is usually
someone around who actually knows how they should be worked.

The *Cross Keys*, at Filance bridge near Penkridge on the northern
part of the canal, typifies the change that has occurred in these pubs
in more recent years. When Rolt found it in 1939 he thought it

(*Top*) The *Holly Bush Inn*, Denford, Caldon Canal; (*Centre*) The *Black Lion*, Consall Forge, Caldon Canal; (*Bottom*) The *Ship*, Levington

Page 126

(*Above*) The *Butt & Oyster*, Pin Mill

(*Below*) The *Old Ship*, Heybridge basin

seemed lost, with its windows 'gazing over the water with pathetic expectancy for boats which never came'. The landlord of the time recalled how every evening boatmen would moor, stable their horses by the pub and spend the night drinking and singing within. Those days were long past; in 1939 only campers used it in the summer, and in winter there was little trade. There are plenty of boats today, and the *Cross Keys* has been modernised inside to cope with the new clientele. Painted ware and harness remind you of the past. From the rear, a housing estate is crawling up towards the pub; this in turn may effect still further change. But at least it is not likely that the *Cross Keys* will become metamorphosed into that monstrous product of the twentieth century, the road house, as has happened elsewhere with results on which it might be libellous to comment.

Unaltered waterside pubs are hard to find, and change, of course, is not necessarily for the worse. Refusal to conform to the whims of fashion and the dictates of commercialism sometimes does elicit admiration, and one of the most admirable canal pubs is the *Bird in Hand* on the Macclesfield Canal, near the hamlet of Kent Green. The Macclesfield, planned by Telford, engineered by William Crosley the younger, was one of the last of the main line canals to be built. It was opened in 1831, and the *Bird in Hand*, apart from the installation of electricity, would be immediately recognisable, inside and out, by any old boatman's ghost who revisited it. It faces a swing bridge, an early nineteenth century house with no architectural pretension whatsoever. Inside there is no bar; the beer, both cool and cheap, comes up from the cellar in a jug and is poured into glasses in the front parlour. You sit and drink in a plain and simple room, with no fruit machine or juke box to waste your money on. For entertainment in the *Bird in Hand* there is conversation: the present landlord is a man of decided views but he is always ready to listen to yours. This, like a handful of other houses—*The Locks* on the Waveney, the *Berkeley Hunt* on the Gloucester & Berkeley Canal, the *Wharf* at Shebdon aqueduct, for example—is a pub of real character with not a trace of the synthetic anywhere about it.

Basins and junctions were focal points for traffic on the canals in the days of commercial carrying. Many of the old basins, especially

H

those in strategic positions near city centres, were filled in when
waterborne trade diminished. Some became car parks, like Dale
Street basin in Manchester, where the Rochdale Canal met the
Ashton. The terminal basin˙ of the Montgomeryshire Canal in
Newtown has been filled in and built over. But where the original
basins survive there is almost always a pub, sometimes more than
one, which in the past would have been busy with boatmen taking
time off after unloading or while waiting for a new cargo.

Despite the fact that what remains is only a part of the great complex of basins lined by warehouses and offices that was the growth
point of the town, Stourport retains what is still one of the most
impressive of canal terminals. Here Brindley's Staffordshire &
Worcestershire Canal locks down to meet the Severn and, although
much of present-day Stourport is a mess, what there is of architectural merit is mostly around the waterside. The river frontage of
the town is dominated by the bulk of the *Tontine Hotel*. A print of
Stourport in 1776 shows the same building much as it looks today.
To one side of it there is a large block of stabling and the building
that is now the *Angel*; behind it there are some warehouses. But
apart from these there is only one house shown in the whole settlement. Today a doctor lives there, but no longer in glorious isola-
tion.

The *Tontine* antedates the Staffs & Worcs Canal by a few years.
As with other hotels of the same name, the money to build it was
raised by the method known as a 'Tontine', which derived from
Italy and is familiar to many who have read Robert Louis
Stevenson and Lloyd Osborne's amusing novel *The Wrong Box*. A
group of fathers put up sums of money which were invested in the
interest of their children. The money remained untouched until all
but one of the children had died. The survivor took the lot. In view
of the trading importance of Stourport in the nineteenth century,
the *Tontine* must have proved a good investment. Now the interior
has something of the air of an old-fashioned railway hotel, where
the trains are infrequent. There are 16 rooms in the pub itself,
which forms the central portion of the building, the remainder con-
sisting of private dwellings with separate entrances. The *Tontine* is
due for interior renovation, but its façade is a piece of waterside
history.

Because they are linked each to each, many of the Midland canals have no elaborate terminal basins. Traffic on the branches or arms, however, the 'no through roads' of the system, went so far and no farther. The Grand Union Canal has several branches: Aylesbury basin has its *Ship Inn*; Buckingham its *Grand Junction Arms*, though the boats stopped coming to Buckingham in 1910 and the basin has long been filled in; and Market Harborough, very busy today with pleasure traffic, has its *Six Packs*. This last house is of true canal origin, as it was built by the Leicestershire & Northamptonshire Union Canal Company who constructed the line from Leicester to Market Harborough, opened in 1809. The pub was originally called the *Union Inn*, and provided extensive stabling. It remained in canal ownership until the 1870s, when it was sold for £1,800 to Henry Hopton, who ran a business on the wharf. In recent years, under brewery ownership, it has been renamed the *Six Packs*. That there is a Union workhouse near by and the 'Six Packs' refers to six packs of local foxhounds is sufficient comment on social pretension. The basin at Market Harborough has come back to life recently with the establishment there of a progressive firm of boat-builders and hirers, so the pub may regret that it has disowned its watery ancestry.

Another canal basin reviving after many years of virtual disuse is at West Stockwith, where the Chesterfield Canal locks down to the Trent. Shared for decades by keels and narrow boats, when commercial traffic stopped in 1955 the basin became a floating grave-yard. Now, trimmed and tidied up, it provides safe harbourage for river cruisers and a smaller number of narrow beam boats that penetrate above Retford on the canal. The *Crown* overlooks West Stockwith basin; it is an uncompromising red-brick building, with two storeys in the front and three at the rear. It used to be very popular with the working boatmen, but the years are taking toll of their numbers. It seems that no, or very few, powered working narrow boats used this canal; if the boatmen had to use the Trent they left their horses at West Stockwith and sometimes hoisted a small sail, to run before the wind.

Chesterfield itself has been inaccessible by canal since 1908, when Norwood tunnel was closed after a roof fall. Worksop, 26 miles from West Stockwith, is the head of navigation, but it lacks a basin and if your craft is more than 30ft long you have to come out in reverse. The little *Canal Tavern* provides some compensation; it is part of a terrace of houses facing the canal as you approach British Waterways Board yard, and Pickford's warehouse straddles the canal a few yards away. The pub, at one time called the *Gas Tavern*, is about the same age as the canal and retains the simple character of the old-fashioned working-man's local. The landlord preserves the pub's long association with the canal and keeps a log-book of all who arrive by boat. It is a journey worth making; the Chesterfield, engineered by James Brindley, is one of the older canals and winds its way through pleasant and varied scenery. Between the *Crown* and the *Canal Tavern* there are ten pubs along its banks, a frequency of refreshment not often met with. They include two *Packet Inns*, one at Retford and the other, forming part of a short but attractive range of early canalside buildings, at Misterton. Above the tunnel at Drakeholes the large *White Swan* seems to be spreading its wings preparatory to take-off. About 200 years old, it has some resemblance to the *Tunnel House* by the Coates portal of Sapperton tunnel; one wonders if it was built for the same reason, to house the tunnel workers, although Drakeholes is only short and cannot have taken much time to cut. The *White Swan* has a large number of rooms and must have been a hotel at some time. The *Chequers* at Ranby retains some of its stabling by the canal, while the *Gate* at Clarborough is a pleasant, small country pub.

On the far side of the Derbyshire hills from the Chesterfield Canal is Whaley Bridge, terminus of the Upper Peak Forest Canal 6 miles from Marple. The *Navigation Inn*, about a hundred years old, can be found in a cluster of buildings a short distance from the basin. This pub used to have one of the smallest bars in the country but was modernised a few years ago. It has kept its old rooftop sign. For the greater part of the canal's working life Whaley Bridge was less important than another terminal at Bugsworth (now known as Buxworth) about a mile away. Here at the end of a short arm of the canal was a whole complex of interchange basins serving the limestone quarries in the hills above. The limestone was brought down by tramroad and either loaded in its containers into the boats or burnt in one of the kilns, of which there were several; 1922 saw the end of this traffic, and the canal arm was abandoned 4 years later.

At Bugsworth there were two pubs, another *Navigation Inn* and the *Rose and Crown*. The latter is now a farmhouse—a reversal of the usual process. The *Navigation*, overlooking the site of the upper-most basin in the complex, survives, a surprisingly lively house considering its position. The stables, warehouses and sheds that used to stand opposite the pub have gone; so has the wheel loading machine which fed the lime into the boats. Light industry flourished here in the past also; the upstairs part of the building adjacent to the pub used to be a riddle works, riddles being sieves. As the industry died in the 1920s, somehow the *Navigation* clung on. The number of regular customers dropped to four a day, and the brewery could no longer afford a landlord. So for a time the *Navigation* was run by an agent who used to arrive by train each morning 'wearing a pot hat and a brolly', and open up. Things are very different now. In 1968 a voluntary organisation, the Inland Waterways Protection Society, began restoration work on the basin area. Progress has been slow but definite and over 600yd of canal has been reinstated.

The importance of Bugsworth, Stourport and the other canal terminals mentioned lies in the past. The Aire & Calder Navigation, however, is still a live commercial waterway and Goole, where it terminates, is very much a viable inland port. As a port, and a town, Goole dates from the 1820s and was wholly a creation of the Aire & Calder Company. Much of the dockland area has been re-structured and the streets of terraced houses have been demolished. Few of the old pubs remain. But Aire Street, the original main street of the town, has been relatively little changed, and the *Lowther Hotel*, the second oldest building in Goole after the church, looks much as it did when the official feast was held here on the opening of the port in 1826. The most noticeable difference would probably have been in its name; the *Lowther Hotel* was built at the expense of Sir Edward Banks, of Joliffe & Banks, principal con-tractors for the port works, and was known as the *Banks Arms*. When Sir Edward died the Navigation Company bought the hotel and in 1835 renamed it the *Lowther*, after Sir John Lowther, the chairman of the company when the navigation was opened. Sir Edward is remembered in Banks Terrace, beside the hotel.

The *Lowther* is a dignified brick building with a stone portico on the top of which used to stand a small cannon, stolen a few years ago on a Sunday and never recovered. Inside it is clearly not what it was, but there is a reminder of former glory in an upstairs room which used to be used for meetings of the Navigation Company. It is a mural painting said to be by a Dutch captain of Goole in its early days showing several sailing ships and river craft and the warehouses and offices of the Ship Dock. Goole's other pubs include the *Vermuyden*, on the Don, otherwise known as the 'Hole in the Wall', the dilapidated *Dock Tavern*, the *Peacock*, the *Cape of Good Hope*, and the *Steam Packet*, although this last has been rebuilt away from its original position. It is a good collection, but only the *Lowther* reflects the assurance of the early nineteenth-century men of industry and commerce.

12

WATERWAYS REVIVED

~~~~~~

As commercial traffic declined, first in the face of railway competition and later with the rapid expansion of road haulage, so many waterways became neglected, disused and, often, legally abandoned. In 1946 the Inland Waterways Association was founded, a group of enthusiasts campaigning for the conservation, development and restoration of the waterway network. Subsequently many local societies were formed to work for the protection and reclamation of the waterways in their own particular area. The efforts of these volunteers, combined with those of the British Waterways Board and of a few enlightened local authorities, have led not only to a revival of public interest in waterways but also to a physical revival of many waterways themselves. The battle is by no means won; no one can accuse central government of being over-generous with public money in this matter and there may be a limit to what can be achieved without far greater financial support. But the picture is very different now from what it was when the IWA began.

The Kennet & Avon Canal is one of the major restoration projects now in hand. This superb waterway, joining Bristol, Bath, Devizes, Newbury and Reading, was the subject of an abandonment proposal by the British Transport Commission defeated in Parliament following great public pressure in 1956. In the last 10 years the Kennet & Avon Trust, working with British Waterways Board, has led the way in bringing the canal back to life. Many locks have been restored and several lengths are now reopened to navigation; Bath City Council have shown the way to other authorities by giving good financial support to the restoration of locks within the city boundaries. That the K & A will be restored throughout there is no doubt; the only question is—by when.

Fewer than twenty pubs survive alongside the 86½ miles of the waterway between Hanham lock, near Bristol, and Reading. In Bristol, the attitude of the Corporation to the development of the docks has given rise to much controversy, but the IWA Water Festivals held in recent years have shown that there is great public interest in their amenity value. One of the remaining dockside pubs is the *Nova Scotia Hotel*, overlooking Cumberland basin. This dates from 1811 and used to have another inn adjacent. For many years Cumberland basin was busy with the Irish cattle trade and within the *Nova Scotia* many bargains were struck. From the wall an iron lamp holder projects 5ft over the pavement; there is a similar one on the *Llandoger Trow*, one of Bristol's best known inns, in King Street. Opposite the *Nova Scotia* on the far side of the cut beneath the old swing bridge there is a row of attractive cottages built by the Dock Company for its workers in 1831. By providing a meeting room for the local branch of the IWA the *Nova Scotia* retains a watery connection which most of Bristol's other pubs have lost.

At Hanham lock the Avon ceases to be tidal. There is a pub with moorings, the *Chequers*, and pubs also by each of the next two locks, the *Swan* at Swineford and the *Jolly Sailor* at Saltford, which has an interesting painting of the Avon in 1726 above the old fireplace. There are no more for the next 9 miles, during which the navigation swings through Bath and ascends the Widcombe flight of locks, most of which have been restored. It will be intriguing to see what happens to Bath Council's proposal to merge two of them together to make one mighty lock with a fall of about 18ft! There is a beautiful cutting through Sydney Gardens where the canal passes beneath two elegant iron footbridges and through two well-proportioned short tunnels with decorated portals; then in about a mile is the *George Inn* at Bathampton and the countryside is reached. The nearest pub to Rennie's magnificent Dundas aqueduct is the *Viaduct Hotel*, which is nearer to the derelict Somersetshire Coal Canal than it is to the K & A, but the next aqueduct at Avoncliff has the seventeenth-century *Crossed Guns* close by. Owing to landslips the canal is dewatered here at this time.

Bradford-on-Avon, something of an architectural treasure-house, is built in terraces rising above the river; the canal has its own small settlement alongside, centred on the lock and bridge. There is a wharf with a dry dock, drained simply by inserting stop planks and pulling out a plug, and a pub, the *Barge*, next to it. Backing on to the water, this is an old canalside house dating from the early nineteenth century. On the town side of the bridge is the *Canal Tavern*, with a wonderful collection of model ships in the bar. The original *Canal Tavern* was the building squeezed in between the towpath and the bridge next door, which still carries the bracket for a hanging sign. The present pub consists of three small old cottages knocked together, the licence being transferred to it when the first *Canal Tavern* passed into private hands. It is an attractive and interesting place and the landlord—as is his fellow at the *Barge*—is a strong supporter of the restoration of the K & A.

By the next wharf, at Hilperton, there is the *King's Arms*, and the second of this canal's *Barge* inns is by the bridge and lock at Seend. This was a farmhouse, and it is not long since the yard was converted into a car park. The *Barge*'s sign shows a painting of Joe Skinner's famous narrow boat *Friendship*, the last of the horse-drawn boats to work the Oxford Canal. Soon the Caen Hill flight of locks, now broken-gated with donkeys grazing in some of the filled-in side ponds, lifts the canal to Devizes, which has its local brewery, Wadworth's, but no canalside pub. The next is the *Bridge* at Horton; thence it is 5 miles to the third of the *Barges*, at Honey Street. Where rags are now made and stored at Honey Street barges used to be built, and a line of cottages faces the canal which was the reason for their existence in this place. Opposite the cottages is the *Barge Inn*, a substantial building side on to the canal. It carries its history on an inscription above the loft door:

> Burnt Dec 12 1858
> Rebuilt in 6 months
> By Samuel Robbins
> Ben Biggs architect.

This seems to have been a dangerous area as it is recorded that part of the wharf was also burnt in 1854, being rebuilt and enlarged the following year. The *Barge* is a mooring point for *Charlotte Dundas*, the K & A Trust's paddle boat which runs public trips on the 'long pound' of the canal.

There is another little canalside village at Pewsey wharf, where pleasure craft are moored and the warehouse is used as a store by BWB. This village also has its pub, the *French Horn*. The 'long pound' continues to Wootton Rivers locks, recently restored and re-opened, on the southern edge of the pleasant village. This length of navigation now ends at Crofton top lock; unfortunately there is no pub here either for boatmen or for the many visitors to the Crofton pumping house, now the property of the Trust, where the restored engines can be seen frequently in steam. Indeed the next pub by the waterside is east of Hungerford, the *Dundas Arms* at Kintbury in between the Kennet and the canal. Charles Dundas, first chairman of the canal company and a member of Parliament for over 50 years, was one of the greatest names in the history of this canal. He lived at Kintbury and is commemorated both in the name of this good little inn and in the finer of Rennie's great aqueducts, near Limpley Stoke.

The canal is navigable from Kintbury through Newbury, but there is only the *White House*, by Swan bridge on the approach to Newbury, to be met with on this stretch. Then there are only four more pubs on the route before the Kennet reaches the Thames. At Aldermaston the bridge no longer swings to let boats interrupt the flow of cars on A340; the turf-sided lock is sadly mouldering, although the *Butt Inn* is busy enough. The fourth of the *Barges*, this one the *Row Barge*, is at Woolhampton; at Burghfield is the *Cunning Man* and in Reading, a few hundred yards from the Thames, the *Fisherman's Cottage*.

The K & A has a fine selection of pubs and it is hoped that they can all remain in business until the whole navigation is reopened, an event which would be accelerated if the County Councils and other local authorities through whose territory the canal passes would take a different view of their responsibilities. That there are County Councils which do take a positive concern is evidenced by recent happenings in the history of the Brecon & Abergavenny Canal, on the other side of the Severn. A few years ago the Monmouthshire and Breconshire County Councils put up equal sums of money, matched in total by BWB, to restore this beautiful canal to full cruising standard. It is true that the B & A has only 6 locks and was never officially closed; but the money was needed if it was to remain in being as a live waterway, and it was forthcoming. When the fixed swing bridge at Talybont was replaced by a lifting bridge in 1970 and navigation was again open to Brecon, the canal was probably as good as ever it had been.

The B & A was cut on a terrace on the hillsides above the Usk; hence for long stretches there are no waterside dwellings and no pubs. The *Royal Oak* in the village of Pencelli is the first from Brecon. The pub was made out of two cottages, about 350 years old, and was first licensed about 1790. As with many other country buildings, ships' timbers were used in the original construction, it being said that the oak returned to the area whence it came when the ships were broken up. Part of the bar room was once stables, with a grain store above. Preserved in the bar is a very old wooden sign, showing a painting of an oak which still exists nearby. The canal runs along the bottom of the garden; bollards on the banks are rejected cannon barrels from the foundry at Dowlais, similar to those that can be found by the course of the filled-in Glamorganshire Canal in Cardiff.

Apart from the *Royal Oak* and the attractive old coaching inn, the *Coach & Horses*, at Llangynidr, the pubs by this canal tend to come in groups. At Talybont, where the canal sits on its terrace level with the roofs of the houses along the road, there are three. The *Star* is probably the oldest; but it, and the *White Hart* and *Traveller's Rest*, probably owes the extent of its premises to the railway rather than the canal age. A meeting is recorded as having been held at the *White Hart* in 1861, as a result of which the Brecon & Merthyr Railway Company agreed to build a carriage bridge over the Usk;

in the same year the canal was bridged, traffic being stopped for only three days, and in 1862 the first locomotive arrived. When the railway was being planned the local paper prophesied that Talybont 'is destined to become, at no great distance of time, a place of great importance ... a railway junction of note—perhaps even a Swindon on a smaller scale'. It never quite happened; now the railway excitement is long over and the boatman is left with three large pubs to choose from in a distance of some quarter of a mile.

The next batch of pubs comes at Gilwern, as Abergavenny is approached. There is one at each end of the bridge: the *Navigation* and the *Bridgend*. Inside, both have been radically treated; only the sign of the *Navigation*, showing a working navvy, retains a canal flavour. In Govilon, the next village, there is another *Bridgend*, small with an attractive frontage, and beneath the aqueduct a *Lion* lurks. Canalside that is all until the junction is reached with the old Monmouthshire Canal at Pontymoile basin, near Pontypool. Much of the Monmouthshire, which once connected with the docks at Newport, is now gone beyond recall, but there are some watered stretches and it is possible to navigate very light craft for nearly 2 miles to Crown bridge, Sebastopol, where reconstruction has produced a bridge-hole more suitable for a tadpole than a boat. But there are two pubs alongside the towpath of the Monmouthshire. One is the *Panteg*, built as a canal pub but deriving most of its trade from the large Panteg works close by. The other, the *Open Hearth*, is a building older than the canal. As trade developed—and the Monmouthshire was a very busy canal in its Victorian heyday, carrying over half a million tons of coal and iron annually down to Newport—the demand grew for places of refreshment, so the *Panteg* was built and the *Open Hearth* converted. When the Monmouthshire Canal & Railway Company was taken over by the GWR the latter pub was called the *Railway*, but it has since taken on its present more hospitable name. The local ironworkers, however, nicknamed it the 'Clout', while they called the *Panteg* the 'Shearers'. BWB draw off a million gallons of water a week for sale to the Panteg Works. IWA working parties use the *Open Hearth* as a headquarters during their efforts to remove from the Monmouthshire the bicycles, mattresses and assorted debris that some of the local inhabitants think it is the fit place for.

Elsewhere in the country two 'circular' navigable routes have been restored and, all being well, both will be busy with boats in 1974. The more southerly circle is a combination of river and canal navigations. It leaves the Severn at Tewkesbury and runs via the Lower Avon to Evesham and along the Upper Avon to Stratford. Thence the south and north sections of the Stratford-upon-Avon Canal climb to King's Norton junction, south of Birmingham, and the Worcester & Birmingham Canal returns you down to the Severn at Worcester, about 20 miles north of the starting point at Tewkesbury. The Lower Avon, part of which had become un-navigable, was rescued after the war by Mr C. D. Barwell, the Lower Avon Navigation Trust and the IWA, with the co-operation of the Severn River Authority. It was fully reopened in 1964. On the Upper Avon work began in 1968 under the leadership of David Hutchings, who had previously led the restoration work on the Southern Stratford Canal. Voluntary labour was used on both these undertakings—if one includes Borstal boys, prisoners from Gloucester gaol and Army engineers as volunteers—and the cost of the works on the Upper Avon will be about £400,000, only £150,000 more than a Government enquiry recommended should be spent on restoring the Upper Avon as long ago as 1920! It may be worth noting the Government contribution to the present scheme is a mere £25,000, just twice as much as the IWA, a voluntary body, has contributed, and one-quarter of the amount given by a single anonymous donor. The navigation was officially reopened in the summer of 1974.

As a result of a campaign led by the Stratford-upon-Avon Canal Society, the heavily locked Southern Stratford Canal escaped official abandonment in 1959, after decades of neglect, and was taken over by the National Trust. It was reopened by the Queen Mother in 1964. The Trust still maintains the canal, although it is an expensive business with three aqueducts and so many locks to be kept in repair. The Southern Stratford meets its northern half at Lapworth, where there is also a connection to the Grand Union Canal. Both sections run through varied and mostly beautiful countryside, but it is the southern section, with its split iron bridges and barrel-roofed lock cottages looking like the cross-section of a tunnel, that has more individuality and charm. From Lapworth around the rest of the circle back to Tewkesbury the waterways have remained in continuous use.

The Lower Avon winds through very pleasant countryside and skirts several villages and the towns of Pershore and Evesham, but there are only two real waterside pubs: the *Fleet*, by the ferry crossing at Twyning, and the *Anchor*, which stands above the river at Wyre Piddle, with its gardens running down to the water's edge. Strictly speaking the Lower and Upper Avon meet at Workman bridge in Evesham, but for restoration purposes the *Bridge Inn* and ferry at Offenham marked the division. The *Bridge* faces the river at the end of a lane; in medieval times there was a stone bridge across the Avon at this point; there was also a ford, this being part of an old highway to London. 'Dead Man's Ait' is the name of the field on the far side of the ferry crossing; here in 1265 took place the Battle of Evesham when Simon de Montfort's army was defeated. There are moorings at the *Bridge*, and a garden by the riverside. There is another pub facing the river on the other side of Offenham—the *Fish & Anchor*, an eighteenth-century building by the roadside. It is possible to walk across the top of the weir at this point to see George Billington lock, named after the man who, knowing he had little time to live, paid for the lock with his savings. The next lock is called Robert Aickman lock after the founder of the IWA, while the lock at Marlcliff is called IWA. Near here is a picture-postcard type pub called the *Cottage of Content*, some yards away from the water.

To facilitate movement of materials by water, a new wharf was made by the *Four Alls* at Binton Bridges. This pub was built as a farmhouse about 1650 and was also the tollhouse for traffic passing over the bridge. The toll-keeper was locally called the Lord of the Isles, after the three islands in the river. The *Four Alls* was licensed about the turn of this century and before the war was known to its frequenters as 'The Knees and Nipples' after the licensee's four nubile daughters. It has recently been tidied up and has a good reputation for food. Boats can navigate the next lock, at Luddington, but thereafter there are problems still to be solved. The lock at Stratford was completed in 1971, a short distance downstream from the Memorial Theatre and the Bancroft basin of the Stratford-upon-Avon Canal. There is another waterside pub on the Avon in

Stratford—the *Hilton Hotel*. If there is ever a prize for the most monstrous of such buildings, this would be a strong contender. In the 13 miles of the Southern Stratford Canal, the last restored segment of this circle, there are only two pubs. At Wootton Wawen, 5 miles from Stratford by the aqueduct constructed, so the memorial plate tells us, in 1813 across what is now the A34, is the *Navigation*, an eighteenth-century building of farmhouse type. For a year or two Wootton Wawen was the termination of the canal, and a basin was built there; horse-drawn waggons completed the route to Stratford, carrying coal at 3s 4d a ton. The connection to Stratford was completed in 1816; it is hard to imagine that the basin in Stratford was once ringed with warehouse and wharf buildings and tramway lines—or indeed that there was not one basin but two. There are 16 locks between Wootton Wawen and Stratford; presumably there was once a pub at Wilmcote nearer the top of the flight, but in any event the *Navigation* was popular with boat crews who used to sleep in what is now the functions room, sometimes bringing their horses in with them.

The other canalside pub is the *Fleur de Lys* at Lowsonford. This is a long, low building, composed of three cottages dating from the thirteenth to fifteenth centuries and incorporating a bakehouse. It is claimed to have been a pub since the fifteenth century and is full of oak beams, brass and copper. Some years ago the Fleur de Lys pies were created here; now they are factory-made and, it is said, have lost their original flavour. The gardens of the pub adjoin the canal; it is a peaceful and beautiful place.

There was a time when it was possible to travel from Stratford to Basingstoke by waterway, via Southern Stratford, Grand Union, Thames, Wey and the Basingstoke Canal. The story of the Basingstoke Canal is one of almost unmitigated financial disaster. It is ironical that one of the few periods in which it did less than badly, as far as receipts were concerned, was when it was carrying materials for the London & Southampton Railway whose competition eventually drove it into liquidation. Subsequently it was bought and sold at various times; Horatio Bottomley had one, or two, hands in it for a couple of years. Since 1949 it has been used as a source of water supply and the condition of much of it is deplorable. Pressure for restoration, however, has been building up for some time, led by the Surrey & Hants Canal Society, and there seems every hope, now that Hampshire County Council have bought their length of canal and Surrey may do likewise, that at least part of the canal will become fully navigable within a few years.

Possibly because the canal, lying between Woking and Basing-stoke, is not remote from centres of population a fair number of its pubs have endured the cessation of commercial traffic. The *Row Barge*, just over 2 miles west of Woking, is one. It was derived from two sixteenth-century cottages; although it is not canalside it is easily accessible along a lane from a point near Goldsworth Top lock, whence boatmen, having moored below the lock, would walk. At Frimley Green the *King's Head* also benefited from the waterway. It is close to the aqueduct carrying the canal over the railway. A nearby house used to be a boathouse owned by the landlord of the pub, where small boats could be hired, and the cottage opposite was once a canalside beerhouse. Neither of these pubs was built especially for the canal trade, unlike the *Fox & Hounds* at Fleet, which faces the towpath and used to have stabling for canal horses adjoining. This pub served those who voyaged the canal for pleasure, in the days when such voyages merited a report in the local newspaper. 21 June 1887 was Jubilee Day, and seven assistants of a 'world-renowned firm of military outfitters in Aldershot' decided to spend the celebrations 'in a quiet and novel manner'. They hired a boat and set off for a three-day canal cruise from the Aldershot boathouse to Odiham. On the first evening they reached the *Fox & Hounds*, described as a 'snug and pretty hostelry', where they refreshed themselves before moving on to pitch camp. They thoroughly enjoyed their outing, as did a gentle-man calling himself 'Musicus' who came from London by train and hired *Gijama*, one of the 'varnished water-tight boats' rented out by Mr H. H. Ulyate, proprietor of the *Fox & Hounds*. Musicus found the Basingstoke Canal 'to bear favourable comparison with many parts of the noble Thames'. He dined in Odiham, but was unable to row farther than North Warnborough on account of the reeds. Nevertheless, he wrote in the *Fleet Monthly Advertiser*, it was 'the most enjoyable day's boating it has ever been my lot to have'. Mr Ulyate hired out six boats altogether and provided for 'Boating,

(*Top*) The *Ferry Boat Inn*, North Fambridge; (*Centre*) The *Jolly Sailor*, Orford;
(*Bottom*) The *Harbour Inn*, Southwold

Page 144

(*Above*) The *Ferry House*, Surlingham

(*Below*) The *Locks*, Ellingham

Fishing, Tea and Picnic Parties'. Perhaps history may be enabled to repeat itself.

At Crookham, west of Fleet, the *Chequers* is close to the bridge of the same name. This house, at least as old as the canal, used to provide lodging by contract for boatmen and stabling for their horses. It was fivepence a night for a man, who had a straw bed above the stable, a clay pipe and a fill of tobacco, but ninepence for a horse, who also got something to eat. A barge tiller on which the horses' harness was hung is preserved in the stable. The *Chequers* is a free house and has been in the same family for well over a hundred years. A cottage close by called The Chestnuts was also a pub once, the *Jolly Waterman*. Boatmen used to take a short cut through the village, leading their horses when they had no barge to pull, rejoining the towpath the other side of the village; this probably explains the name given to this one-time pub. Another pub which provided lodgings for boatmen was the *Swan* at North Warnborough; they used a back bedroom reached by its own staircase.

The Basingstoke Canal has one long tunnel, Greywell, 1,200yd. Part of it fell in in 1932, thus cutting off Basingstoke from the rest of the waterway. The *Fox & Goose* is near the eastern portal and the end of the horse path over the tunnel top. The inn certainly dates from the nineteenth century and must have been used by the leggers while waiting for, or recovering, from business. In Basingstoke itself the *Barge Inn* and the *Railway Inn*, both of which served the canal, have gone, but a new pub, the *Goat & Barge*, was opened in 1970—a 'thematic' pub, canal life providing the theme. It may be phony, the Basingstoke having been a barge canal rather than one extensively used by narrow boats, but it is fun—which is more than can be said for the chrome and plastic decor favoured by brewers' architects from time to time in the mid-twentieth century.

Waterway restoration is not confined to the southern half of the country. The Caldon Canal, which branches off from the Trent & Mersey at Stoke-on-Trent, is now being put back into working order with the help of a grant of £50,000 from Stoke-on-Trent and Staffordshire County Council. Wedged in between the two arms of this canal, one leading toward Leek and the other to a basin at Froghall, and close to the Hazelhurst aqueduct is the small yellow-washed *Holly Bush Inn*, on the end of a short terrace of cottages.

Within a couple of miles is the canal world in miniature; road and accommodation bridges, a lift bridge, locks, a tunnel and the aqueduct itself taking one arm of the canal over the other. Modernisation has scarcely affected the *Holly Bush*, which consists of two small rooms containing some interesting old photographs of the canal and its people of the past. Another small low-ceilinged pub is the *Boat* at Basford bridge near Cheddleton, where the landlord dislocated his shoulder while undertaking a one-man restoration effort of clearing out an old landing stage below the pub. Unlike the *Holly Bush* the *Boat* antedates the canal, but it is said always to have been a pub.

The pride of the Caldon pubs, however, must be the *Black Lion* at Consall Forge. When the forge was in operation, about 2,000 men were employed in the area; the *Black Lion* served them, as well as travellers who arrived by rail and the boatmen from the canal. In less hurried days engine drivers would stop for a pint in hot weather; now there are few trains and the nearby railway station has been closed. Without a permit from the local estate there is no access for vehicles to the *Black Lion*, and you have to earn your drink by walking down from the hills on either side. On the eastern side is the Devil's Staircase; on the west three fields have to be crossed, 204 steps descended, then over the River Churnet, the canal and the railway and up to the pub. But not to the original pub, which was a small stone building a few yards away from the present *Black Lion*, now used as an outhouse. The *Black Lion* is plain enough, making no concessions to the picturesque. Inside the bar floor is flagged and there is a small smoke room with a photograph of the canal in Edwardian times. The Churnet valley and the *Black Lion* are popular with walkers, and there are more dwellings, and drinkers, hidden in the trees than might at first be thought. But even the reopening of this stretch of the canal will not altogether restore to the *Black Lion* the full vigour of its past.

North-eastward, in Yorkshire, two connecting waterways, one natural and one artificial, are now being brought back to navigable standards. The attractive Pocklington Canal, with its substantial and elegant brick bridges, is publess along its length; on the south side of Pocklington at Canal Head, however, the windows of the *Wellington Oak* look out over the A1079 to the old warehouses beside the canal basin. At its western end the canal meets the York-shire Derwent near the village of East Cottingwith. Throughout most of the eighteenth and nineteenth centuries the Derwent was quite a busy trading river, but its business declined sharply after the opening of the York–Scarborough railway line in 1845. Nine years later Earl Fitzwilliam, whose family had been long connected with both the river and the canal, sold the navigation to the North Eastern Railway. Trade continued to decline and the condition of the 5 locks on the Derwent to deteriorate. The last trader to use the navigation was Mr J. W. Brown of Bubwith; he was carrying coal up the river in the early 1900s and made the final voyage in his barge *Ebenezer* in 1932. Although it seemed in subsequent years that all was lost, after years of negotiation the Yorkshire Derwent Trust and the Ouse River Authority agreed on a programme of restora-tion, and the lowest lock, at Sutton, was reopened in 1972. The intention is to restore the navigation to Malton and to build a barrage, incorporating a lock, at the river's junction with the Ouse, rendering the Derwent non-tidal. Including the Pocklington Canal, this will give a length of 47½ miles of scenically varied and interesting waterway.

On the Derwent, as on the Yorkshire Ouse as well, bridges were by no means numerous. Two of the surviving Derwentside pubs used to be ferry houses. At the end of a track at Breighton, near Bubwith, is the *Half Moon Inn*, which has had a modern frontage added to a building that looks well over 200 years old. This is a friendly house with every facility, that has 'moved with the times' as it were, without descending into vulgarity. The other ferry house is the *Ferry Boat Inn* at West Cottingwith, across the river from the junction with the canal. It used to be a condition of the tenancy that the licensee operated the ferry between West and East Cottingwith, used by villagers on the eastern side travelling to York via the horse bus from Thorganby which ran twice a week. The inn, a plain little house at the end of a lane overlooking the river, was part of the Thicket Priory Estate. The ferry ended its run in the early 1940s, demand having fallen off and the boat being no longer riverworthy. Sir John Dunnington-Jefferson, who then owned the estate, relieved the *Ferry Boat*'s tenant of his ferrying obligation.

The *Ferry Boat Inn* may be as much as 400 years old. It was modernised in 1947, but features of the old building are still evident. It had its own brewhouse, demolished a few years ago. It was a popular call for bargemen—as it now is for fishermen—who used to sit and drink outside around the barrels by the brewhouse. Near the inn there used to be one of at least three wooden drawbridges that spanned the Derwent within a few miles. One of these Dutch-type bridges, familiar to those who know the paintings of Van Gogh, has been dismantled and is in store in York awaiting a place in a proposed open-air museum. The bridge near the *Ferry Boat* may have been used for the collection of tolls from passing boats. It cannot have been a very useful alternative to the ferry as to get to West Cottingwith would have meant having to cross the canal lock as well—not an easy matter when loaded down with shopping from the market or beer from the *Ferry Boat*.

Other Yorkshire waterways where the restoration of navigation is a strong and practical possibility are the Driffield Navigation and the Ripon Canal. Driffield has a superb basin; all it lacks, unfortunately, is a waterside pub. The basin at Ripon is also interesting, there still being evidence of the separate little coal wharves. Nearby is the *Navigation Inn*. In all, there are over thirty inns and hotels called the *Navigation*; two more of them are alongside the Lower Peak Forest Canal, which has recently been restored. Now this and the Ashton Canal are reopened a circular route, the 'Cheshire Ring', of about a hundred miles is once again available to boats. There is yet another *Navigation*, by Beswick locks on the Ashton; also a less usually named pub, the *Crabtree*, half way up Clayton locks at Openshaw.

In view of the change in public attitude and sudden outbursts of local enthusiasm it is becoming unwise these days to speak of any abandoned or derelict waterway as being beyond recall. There is talk of reopening parts of both the Wey & Arun Junction, abandoned in 1868, and the Portsmouth & Arundel which, apart from the Chichester branch, was abandoned in 1896. Pubs which played some part in the history of these undertakings may soon be selling beer to thirsty members of working parties. One of them is the *Three Compasses*, which stands on the corner of a minor road on the west side of A281 at Alfold Crossways in Surrey. Here the Earl of

Egremont presided at a celebration before the inaugural voyage on the Wey & Arun Junction in 1816. Four miles south on B2133 at Loxwood is the *Onslow Arms*, a good base from which to examine the remains of a Wey & Arun lock. Having completed one's tour of the Wey & Arun one can follow the winding course of the river through Arundel to Ford station. Close by is the *Ship and Anchor*, a modernised house with a marina incorporating the entrance to the Portsmouth & Arundel Canal. The course of this canal passes through Yapton on A2024 by a pub which has claims to the longest name of any in the British Isles, the *Shoulder of Mutton and Cucumbers*. It is likely that both the house and its name antedate the waterway as sauce made from cucumbers was an eighteenth-century speciality in this part of the country.

However, it may be too much to hope that it will ever again be possible to travel through the countryside by boat from London to Portsmouth as it was for a few years in the early nineteenth century. Likewise, although it endured far longer, the Thames–Severn link may never be re-established. The last portion was abandoned in 1933 and, although almost the whole line is easily discernible, the problems of restoration are enormous. The inland port of Brims-combe, where goods from Severn trows were trans-shipped into barges for the Thames, is now a factory site. The name of the *Ship Inn* gives a clue to the transport history of the area; it stands beside the line of the canal on the west side of what was the port, a small and pleasant village pub. At Chalford, 1½ miles east, is the *Red Lion*, which has given its name to the lock nearby. Above the *Red Lion* is the *Valley Inn*, which used to be a millowner's house. It stands by a bridge on the outskirts of the village, about 2 miles from the point where the canal reaches its summit level at Daneway. The top lock has disappeared beneath the car park of the *Daneway Inn*. West of the road bridge here there used to be a basin and a warehouse. The present inn was built for the canal company in 1784, becoming a pub a few years later with the name of the *Bricklayer's Arms*. Before then it had served as a lodging house for the gangs working on Sapperton tunnel; once licensed it served the boatmen before or after their ordeal of a 2-mile underground voyage. The old name was a reminiscence of the time when bricks for use in lining the tunnel were burnt near the house. Newspaper cuttings about various attempts to navigate the tunnel in more recent years can be found inside, but can scarcely be read in summer, the size of the car park betraying the popularity of the inn. The crumbling western portal of Sapperton is a short walk along the overgrown towpath from the inn. Close to the portal is a small building which was a beerhouse when the tunnel was first used in 1789.

Above Sapperton's east portal is the *Tunnel House*, originally the *New Inn* and built for the same purpose as the *Daneway* at the other end. Most of the tunnellers were miners from different parts of the country and part of the innkeeper's duty was to keep an eye on them. In 1952 much of the building was destroyed by fire; it has been well and tactfully restored but as a two-storey house. The old third storey used to be a dormitory; the floor below was also used for sleeping quarters but was divided into rooms. On the ground floor some of the original beams survived the fire. Recent alterations have revealed a fireplace in what may have been a bakehouse in the building's earlier years. The *Tunnel House* is not only historically waterside; in its deep, tree-lined cutting the canal still holds some water.

Here and there in England and Wales there are other public houses which were once waterside but are so no longer. At Camerton, in what used to be Somerset mining country, is the *Jolly Collier* inn; behind it is the line of the Somersetshire Coal Canal, abandoned in 1904. By the basin of the Thames & Medway Canal at Gravesend is a *Canal Tavern*. Within ¼ mile of the *Canal Inn* south of Wrantage on A378 is the site of an aqueduct, the remains of an inclined plane and the north portal of Crimson Hill tunnel on the Chard Canal. The pub sign shows, optimistically but inaccurately, a narrow boat; the Chard was a tub-boat canal. Not so far away, to the west of Taunton, the *Victory Inn* in the hamlet of Allerford is a useful landmark for anyone seeking the site of the Hillfarrance lift (sometimes known as the Victory) on the Grand Western Canal. The western section of this waterway has been reopened for un-powered craft but the eastern half has been abandoned since 1867 and only remnants are traceable. In Leicestershire, Melton Mowbray has a *Boat Inn* in Burton Street, beside what used to be the basin shared by the Oakham Canal and the Melton Mowbray

Navigation. The *Rutland Arms*, north of Woolsthorpe near Grantham, is part of what was a small canalside settlement by the Grantham Canal, although in this case the canal is still watered and is a likely candidate for restoration before many years. The poor old Derby Canal is still remembered by a *Navigation Inn* at Breaston; the equally unfortunate Wisbech Canal is landmarked by two pubs regal in nomenclature but otherwise unexceptional, the *Royal Standard* and the *Prince of Wales*. In the north there is a *Jolly Sailor* where the A638 crosses the line of the Barnsley Canal near Wakefield, a *Summit Inn* by the summit level of the Rochdale Canal on A6033, and in the north-west the Ulverston Canal has a *Canal Tavern* at one end and a *Bay Horse* at the other, with water, but no navigation, in between. In South Wales the northern section of the Swansea Canal can be examined in the vicinity of three pubs on the A4067: the *Castle Hotel*, the *Yniscedwyn Arms* and the *Aubrey Arms*. Finally on the old course of the Glamorganshire Canal at Abercynon the *Navigation House* used to overlook one of the most important traffic junctions in South Wales, a basin where a tramroad from Gelligaer and the famous Penydarren tramroad from Dowlais, on which Trevithick's first locomotive ran in 1804, both terminated. Here the canal crossed the Taff by an aqueduct on the line of the present road bridge and the coal and iron were loaded on to the boats by the *Navigation House* for the journey to Cardiff.

13

EAST COAST RIVERS

~~~~~~

More than half of the one-inch Ordnance Survey sheet 150 (Ipswich) is taken up by water. Much of this water is inland—the wide estuaries of the Suffolk rivers, Deben, Orwell, Alde and Ore, and, shared with Essex, the Stour. The riversides have a fine, although not large, collection of pubs, many of them ferry houses dating back several centuries. Most are well-frequented, especially in the summer months, by yachtsmen, holidaymakers and their own local clientele, but on the whole they have escaped the more disastrous effects of modernisation.

Because of subsidence the Deben has an outsize estuary compared to the little river which feeds it. The bar across its mouth has always kept the larger ships away, and Woodbridge was never a port to rival Ipswich. On the southern side of the river mouth was the medieval port of Goseford, which would have been flourishing at the time the Felixstowe ferry was first recorded as operating, in 1181. This ferry, across the river to Bawdsey, still operates; the old ferry house must have been near, if not actually where, the present

Ferry Boat Inn stands behind the shingle bank containing the river. This is itself a very old house, fifteenth or sixteenth century, with low ceilings and massive oak beams. Edward Fitzgerald, a Woodbridge man, the translator of the *Rubaiyat* of Omar Khayyam, often visited the *Ferry Boat* in his schooner *Scandal* (its name his comment on the chief occupation of Woodbridge society) where presumably he would

> '. . . fill the Cup that clears
> Today of past Regrets and Future Fears . . .'

In 1882 Sir Cuthbert Quilter completed the building of his heart's desire, Bawdsey Manor, one of the most splendidly appalling of all Victorian country houses. A few years later he had the ferry brought up to date by introducing two steam vessels running via chains laid across the river to keep them on course. This lasted for about 30 years but with insufficient demand and increasing costs was abandoned in the 1920s in favour of a rowing boat. Later a motor boat took over. Sold to the government in 1936, Bawdsey Manor became the headquarters of the team developing what was first known as radio-location and then as radar; the *Ferry Boat Inn* became the 'local' for RAF personnel based at the Manor during the war and there were many interesting ferry journeys back to Bawdsey after closing time.

There are two pubs upriver towards Woodbridge: the *Ramsholt Arms* on the east bank and the *Maybush* at Waldringfield on the west. The *Ramsholt Arms* was a ferry house in the seventeenth century. Later it became a farmhouse called the Dock Farm, after the small Ramsholt dock next to it. The third house up the hill from the dock, now a private dwelling, was the *Dock Inn* and has large cellars beneath it. At some time the *Dock Inn* closed and the farm began selling beer to the handful of local watermen and the occasional visitor. With Mrs Nunn as landlady, customers would help themselves to their beer and add up their own bills at the end of the evening. Old George Cook would sit in the corner, smoking out customers he did not like with his home-made tobacco. Things are different now, more in keeping with the twentieth century possibly. But despite the twentieth century this is still a beautiful place; most of the fabric of the old building is preserved in the present pub, and the quay where hay used to be loaded on to Walter Wrinch's barges is still there for the yachtsman's use.

There was also a ferry at Waldringfield, and the landlord doubled as ferryman in the later nineteenth century. But the oldest part of the *Maybush* dates from much earlier, possibly from the fifteenth century. Originally a very small house built of narrow bricks it was the *Cliff Inn* about 1800. It has been extended since the war and is now very popular with the holiday crowds, many seeking refuge from the night life of Felixstowe. There is a caravan site adjacent, yachts and dinghies bobbing in the river; a holiday scene in microcosm. It is hard to realise that this used to be a Suffolk industrial centre with twelve kilns baking chalk and mud to make cement. Frank Mason, who owned the factory, also ran a fleet of seven barges from Waldringfield, trading to London and Ipswich. The factory closed in 1907 and was demolished in succeeding years. The barges were sold, the last survivor, the *Orinoco*, being sunk in 1966. As so often, the pub, like the church, is the link between past and present; the ceiling spinner in the bar must have been twirled time and time again by Mason's barge captains and crews on an evening between trips.

Woodbridge itself used to boast a formidable list of waterside inns, all appropriately named: the *Boat*, the *Ship*, the *Mariner's Arms*, the *Ocean Monarch* and the *Anchor*. The last named is the only quayside pub left. In his fascinating study of the Deben, *Suffolk Estuary*, W. G. Arnott quotes a party song sung at leave taking when a ship left port:

'The Boat, Ship and Anchor
Was the Englishman's boast
If you'll call at these houses
They'll give you a toast . . .

May the Anchor hold fast
And the Boat safely swim
And the sails of the Ship
Always keep trim . . .'

Do men these days, one wonders, ever compose songs in honour of their local public houses?

Although Woodbridge as a port did little more than languish and die in the age of steamships, the quayside was busy for centuries with sailing barges and is still busy with yachts. Sailing barges served the Tide Mill, Woodbridge's most famous building. The existence of the Tide Mill was first recorded in 1170, the first mention of one anywhere in the country. The present structure probably dates from the late seventeenth century. It is the only example left that can be restored, as indeed is now happening thanks to the Woodbridge Tide Mill Trust. Sadly, in its last years of operation the machinery of the mill was converted to diesel power, but when restoration is completed the wheel will again revolve, if only for demonstration purposes, to the power of the tides.

The Orwell, which is the estuary of the Gipping, is rather wider and grander than the Deben. The growth of Ipswich and the proximity of main roads to its banks are not to its advantage, although it still preserves a comparable beauty to its neighbour. The Orwell, with no bar at its mouth and with plenty of water, was for centuries a busy trading river and Ipswich is recorded as a centre of boat building since 1295. Surprisingly, the estuary had few ferries; it also has few pubs. There is a well-known one west of the centre of Felixstowe at Walton, where river walls and land reclamation have left the old *Ferry Boat Inn* surveying a clutter of building works and parking lots for heavy lorries. This inn, best known as 'The Dooley', which name is said to originate from the word 'dole', meaning a boundary path, was built as a ferry house in the late fifteenth century and obtained a licence about 1838 with the landlord, as in many other places, doubling as ferryman. Before the walls were built it was possible for passengers to be landed at high tide at the door of the inn. The ferry, known in its earlier years as the Wagtaile Ferry from a house near to it with that name, sailed to Harwich. There was a creek on the Walton side, and a jetty; the outline of the entrance to the creek can be seen on the OS map. Like other creeks on the East Coast estuaries, this was a haunt of smugglers. And, like other pubs in the same area, the 'Dooley' has a remarkably large number of doors inside, far more than the number of rooms the building would appear to contain. Both smugglers and dodgers of the press gang found these doors useful when pursuit drew nigh. Recent extension has altered the interior of the pub to some extent, but it is still a plain and homely place with plenty of wood about, beer drawn from barrels and a ceiling spinner similar to that in the *Maybush* on the Deben.

There is no pub on the riverside between Walton and Ipswich, but there is one with such close connections to the water that it cannot be ignored. The *Ship* stands next to the church in the small village of Levington, nearly half way along the estuary. It has been a pub since 1723, though the building itself dates from the 1570s, and is opposite to the top of the path leading down to Levington Creek, a path used by the pilots on their way to pick up the Thames barges which traded from London to this river. Incoming cargoes included bricks, and manure from the London slums for use on the farms. Corn was taken to London, though not, one hopes, in the same barges that had brought a less savoury cargo, and coprolite (red crag full of fossilised animal bones) which was of high value as a fertiliser was exported in great quantities during the nineteenth century from the Orwell and the Deben. Peat and turf were other important outward cargoes.

When the railway opened, the pilots used to walk to the *Ship* from the nearest station, have their bread and cheese and beer and then stroll down the path to await their craft. Since those days, the *Ship* has changed very little. The external timbers of the building are concealed by dark grey stucco, but inside the small pub there is a wealth of oak, with the stem of a ship built into the fabric. The house is thatched, and the small rooms are still numbered according to the old customs and excise regulations. The main room is furnished with old wooden high-backed settles; as a reminder that we are in a farming area 'God Speed The Plough' is carved on the back of one. God is also called on to 'Save the old Ship and all her Crew' in a notice in raised lettering framed upon the wall. There are convenient ledges at shoulder height for those who prefer to take their drink on their feet, and the paintwork and ceiling are stained a dark tobacco brown. The present landlord, Mr Nunn, has resisted all attempts to modernise the pub; the only concession to the advance of technology is electric light, and not too much of that. Mr Nunn is critical about the probability of the vessel painted on the flaking sign outside, and says how much he preferred its predecessor, 'a real ship'. For many years the pub had no sign, and needed none; it is still one of the very few houses which has not got the brewers' name emblazoned outside—and all praise to them for that. It is also another of the very few houses where the beer comes straight from the barrel. There is a direct simplicity about the *Ship* which is met with seldom in public houses, whether waterside or not.

There used to be an *Anchor* at Nacton and a *Wherry Inn* in Ipswich, opposite Stoke, existing in 1800 although the Norfolk wherry, if that is what it was named after, was not a usual craft in this river. On the southern side is the *Ostrich* at Bourne bridge. The inn and bridge are both of medieval origin; the *Ostrich* derives its name from the crest of Lord Chief Justice Coke in the early 1600s.

The only pub on the Orwell that has its feet really in the water is the *Butt & Oyster* at Pin Mill. A mill is recorded here in the fourteenth century and the *Butt & Oyster* has been a pub since 1558, much of the building dating from that time. Like Waldringfield, this was a place once busy with local industry. Apart from the mill itself, there was a salt pan here in the Middle Ages; boats were built and repaired here and there was a stone works served by some fifty boats. Now it is one of the most popular moorings on the East Anglian rivers. A long hard stretches over 200yd into the Orwell and at low tide you have to walk all of that distance from your boat. But at high tide you may be able to tie up to one of the rings fixed to the wall of the pub and have your beer passed to you through the window. The name of the pub is a matter for argument; the Butt may be an oyster butt, a flounder, or a reference to an archer's target, archery having been practised in a field nearby. It is said to have been popular with smugglers and was certainly popular with the crews of sailing vessels which used to moor a little downstream in Butterman's Bay. Half a dozen sailing barges still moor by the *Butt & Oyster*, stting flat in the mud at low water. The building has been extended and refaced; inside the oak beams have been plastered over. Nevertheless, even in this age of the motor car it remains very much a waterman's pub.

The last pub by the Orwell is the *Bristol Arms* at Shotley, close to the naval establishment HMS *Ganges*. From the windows there is a fine view of Harwich and Parkeston quay but the building itself has been refronted and renovated and has little individuality about it. It also began its life as a ferry house, belonging to the Lord of the

Manor, and the hard-working tenant had to run both the ferry and a farm as well as keep the inn.

Round the corner from Shotley is the estuary of the Stour, with far more mud than water and no shelter for the sailor until he can get into Mistley. Once Parkeston quay is passed, it is a lonely place from the water. Mistley was once a port of some importance but was overtaken by its upstream neighbour Manningtree which, when the navigation of the river from Sudbury was improved following an Act of 1705, became a trans-shipment port served by barges of the type made famous by the paintings of Constable. Mistley came again into prominence later in the century when the owner of the estate, Richard Rigby, employed the renowned architect Robert Adam to transform the old place into a port and spa. Trade was encouraged and arrived, and in the Napoleonic Wars warships were built at Mistley. Later the farming family of the Horlocks moved in, buying and building barges and bringing prosperity to the riverside. Little is left now of Robert Adam's Mistley, though one can hardly miss the Towers and the decorative —or comical—swan sitting in its little round pond in front of what used to be the spa pavilion. It is not much more than the relic of a port. The malthouses, however, those dating from 1807 contrasting with the big range built for Brooks in 1901, still recall one of the principal items of waterborne trade. The old waterside *Grapevine* has closed, but there is a pub called the *Thorn*—this was the old name given to the Mistley waterside—and the *Anchor* stands on a hill above the river. In neighbouring Manningtree two inns, the *Crown* and the *White Horse*, have yards leading to the river, and the *Skinner's Arms*, an old favourite with the crews of sailing barges, is nearby. While in this area it is worth remarking that at Lawford, a mile or so away, there used to be a lady blacksmith.

The Stour upstream of the tidal lock at Brantham is one of the most beautiful of all rivers. So many of the subjects of Constable's paintings belong to the Stour: Flatford Mill, Willy Lott's cottage, the church towers seen across the river, the leaping horse, the locks, the barges. 'The sound of water escaping from mill-dams, willows, old rotten planks, slimy posts and brickwork, I love such things,' he wrote. 'These things made me a painter, and I am grateful.' Unfortunately, in the history of the Stour navigation, as of so many others, there are too many 'old rotten planks'; it is much the same on too many canals today. Many of the Stour's locks are unusable and some are virtually non-existent, although four have been rebuilt and it may be possible to move craft by rollers around the barrage which the River Authority intend to build. The River Stour Trust are trying to preserve the riverside scene and to develop navigational possibilities; they have recently succeeded in raising and restoring one of the old barges, or lighters, sunk in a cut near Sudbury.

Two miles south of Sudbury, in the small village of Henny Street, is one of the old Stourside bargemen's pubs, the *Swan*. It is separated from the river by the width of the road and a stretch of grass. There used to be a lock here but, like the mill in the village, it has gone. The *Swan* is a plain brown roughcast building of two storeys, the roughcast presumably concealing plenty of oak as the pub dates from 1600. In the present car park there used to be a blacksmith's forge; many of the cars belong to anglers, possibly believers in the landlord's story that the fish on this stretch of water will not bite during opening hours.

The *Anchor* at Nayland was another bargemen's pub; its car park is on the site of a wharf. The *Anchor* is close to the rather ugly modern bridge over the river; built in 1959, this bridge replaced an early eighteenth-century hump-backed bridge, which in turn had replaced a timber bridge built in the early sixteenth century by a local clothier, William Abel. The present construction has an old stone plaque from its predecessor bearing the rebus, a bell with an A on it, of this local benefactor, who also paid for the porch of the church and lived in a beautiful house, Alston Court, in the centre of this most attractive village. When the hump-backed bridge was being demolished, a cache of explosives was discovered, enough to blow up half the village, which had been put there during the war in case of invasion and had been forgotten.

Nayland was a cloth-making centre and retains several old weavers' cottages. At one time it had thirteen pubs. The *Anchor* was firstly the *King's Head*, built in 1753, being renamed four years later for some undiscoverable reason. It became the headquarters of a naval press gang during the Napoleonic Wars—presumably trying to raise men for the ships built downriver at Mistley. It was burnt down in the late nineteenth century and was moved a little nearer to the river on rebuilding. Though it is late Victorian, the pink-washed, clean-looking *Anchor* harmonizes well with the rest of the village. It even carries an anchor as its sign, instead of a picture of one.

Southwards from the Stour is the Colne, with Colchester at the head of the estuary. There is half a mile of quayside at Colchester Hythe, looking in good order and only waiting for vessels to use it, of which there are few. There are timber yards and modern warehouses of stupendous ugliness. Wedged in amongst them is the *Maltsters Arms*, cut off from the water by one of the warehouses. It has a well-painted sign showing an impressive brick-built maltings which must have made an aesthetic as well as practical contribution to the area when it stood there. The *New Dock Inn* is another little pub in the port area, facing the road running parallel to the quay. Fleets of sailing barges used to work out of Colchester and a few were still trading until after the last war but today the river does not seem an integral part of the town, each appearing to avoid the other. Perhaps this was always so.

Wivenhoe, separated from Colchester by the University of Essex, is very much of a waterside place. The building and repairing of yachts is a major activity; the quayside is always colourful and usually busy. From the far side of the river Wivenhoe looks too good to be true. One looks in vain for the gimcrack shops, the fish and chippery, the plastic gaudiness which so often disfigure the 'beauty spot'. Here is a group of buildings which seem to fall into a natural harmony, such as one finds frequently in Holland but seldom in Britain. In the middle of the group is a small inn, the *Crown & Anchor*, about 300 years old, remodelled inside without being devastated and making a comfortable companion for its neighbours on the waterfront. A bend in the river conceals Wivenhoe from Rowhedge on the west bank of the Colne; so instead of being able to admire the scene from the garden or windows of the *Anchor* one has to take a lonely path to the ferry landing a mile from Fingringhoe, near where the Roman River joins the Colne. Rowhedge is workmanlike rather than beautiful. The *Anchor*, more than two centuries old, backs on to the waterside. Like the *Crown & Anchor* it is a cosy pub. Divisions between the rooms inside have been removed; some timbers are exposed and what can only have been a mast runs the length of the building from front to back.

South of Mersea Island is the wide estuary of the Blackwater. On the north side approaching Maldon, Heybridge basin, designed by John Rennie, marks the entrance to the Chelmer & Blackwater Navigation, which leads to Chelmsford through 13 locks. A variety of interesting craft can usually be found moored in the canal. A pink-washed eighteenth-century pub, the *Old Ship*, stands by the sea lock at the end of a row of very attractive weather-boarded cottages facing the canal. Not many people would visit Heybridge basin unless they were connected with boats and the walls of the bar are covered with framed photographs of sailing barges, yachts and dinghies. The *Old Ship* bears a Viking longboat on its sign, token of the old history of Danish invasion. Fifty yards from the *Old Ship*, beneath the river wall, the green-washed *Jolly Sailor* continues the nautical theme. Two waterside pubs in the same small place while most of the other riverside settlements in Essex and Suffolk have either one or none is indicative of the custom brought by the canal. The Chelmer & Blackwater Navigation was not nationalised with the great majority of other waterway undertakings and is still an independent concern.

There are two pubs also by the quay in Maldon, another *Jolly Sailor*, a blue one this time, an intriguing building with windows all over the place and a look-out window on the top, and the *Queen's Head* on the Hythe, modernised within but with the line of the roof showing its age. Maldon is another mooring for Thames sailing barges; *King*, *Kimberley*, *Lady Gwynford*, *Dawn*, *Marjorie*, *Ardwina*, *Beatrice Maud* and *Northdown* were lying there one day in 1973, and *Kitty*, built 1895, was available on charter. According to Hervey Benham, author of *Down Tops'l* which tells in invigorating language the story of the East Coast sailing barges, the 'loveliest barge ever built', *Record Reign*, came from the yard of Howard of Maldon. This was the home of the stackies, barges built to take cargoes of hay and straw, veritable haystacks afloat, which traded up London river. Maldon Hythe, though not perhaps the town, is fascinating still; with Hervey Benham's book at hand you can look up the history of the barges moored there, several of which are likely to date from the nineteenth century, tangible evidence of the

K

Blackwater's—and the other East Coast rivers'—trading history.

A particularly good old inn is 6 miles south of Maldon across country, though a great deal farther by water; the *Ferry Boat* at North Fambridge on the River Crouch. Dating from 1486 this is a white weather-boarded house, with small rooms containing a host of interesting objects. It is 250yd from the ferry landing; the ferry no longer operates but the winch and coils of wire are rusting by the slipway. The inn is protected by the river wall and is only literally waterside at very high tides when the water edges its way up the road from the ferry landing. This bit of riverside has its own romantic episode. Lady Frances Rich fell in love with John Cammock, whose family was lower than hers in the social order. Her father caught them out of doors and unawares; they both leapt on John's horse, fled to the river, swam over from South to North Fambridge and thence rode to Maldon, where they married and went on to produce thirteen children.

Another East Coast pub not literally waterside today but which owes its existence to the water lies some distance to the north—the *Jolly Sailor* at Orford. It is near the Alde, a strange river that winds its way to Snape, with its famous maltings, where it becomes navigable, opens up into the Long Reach, with wide mud flats on either side, dodges around Aldeburgh and then turns west of south to run parallel with the coast and often within only a few hundred yards of it until, having passed Orford, it becomes the River Ore and emerges into Hollesley Bay with a difficult shingle bar at its mouth. This is a shifting coastline; the North Sea which higher up the coast has eaten away the old port of Dunwich, has bitten off a good part of Aldeburgh, consumed the port of Slaughden within the past century or so with its boat-building yards and *Three Mariners* inn, and pushed up the long bank of shingle known as Orford Bench. It is a place of keen winds and a sanctuary for wild birds. Orford was a port since about the ninth century; its castle was built by Henry II and the size of its church indicates the wealth of the township under the Tudors, when wool was exported overseas. In the reign of Victoria the quayside was busy with shallow-draught barges. It is only since then that the *Jolly Sailor* has ceased to be waterside, as it stands on what used to be the quay and boats would load and unload in a basin, now a car park, opposite. The floods of

1953 put the water back into the basin for a time. Apart from castle and church, other relics of Orford's old glory remain, including the Regalia and the Town Charter, but to the visitor, who may well have only come to the place for a meal at the famous Butley Oysterage, there is a certain air of unreality prevalent. What do people do here; what is the place for; and what happens over the river at Orfordness? There are answers, but they are not immediately apparent. Orford seems to be waiting for something to happen. One hopes it will not happen, because in such cases the happening is likely to be 'development' of some kind or another for some commercial purpose, perhaps connected with the 'holiday industry', more likely to destroy than to enhance the beauty that is left.

The *Jolly Sailor* is mainly a seventeenth-century house, said to have been built with the timbers from wrecked ships. Upstairs is a mural discovered under sixteen layers of wallpaper, showing a number of fully rigged sailing vessels. There used to be a handbill calling for the arrest of Margaret Catchpole, heroine of a famous Suffolk smuggling story, part fact, part fiction, written by the Revd Richard Cobbold in 1846. There are eight doors in one room and two cupboards—enough to give credence to smuggling yarns even if historical documentation is lacking. There are also the 'Little Dogs of Orford', a stuffed group of miniature pug-like animals in a glass case, whose origin is uncertain. The inn has three public rooms; the taproom, which used to be the kitchen, a saloon and a room added in 1932 for the oyster feasts. The old oyster beds, however, were dredged up before the war. The landlords of the *Jolly Sailor* can be traced back to 1839; the best known of them, Steve Harper, had his portrait painted by T. C. Dugdale and hung in the Royal Academy. Among the better known frequenters of more recent years was Sir Robert Watson-Watt, who was working on the Ness on the development of radar before moving to continue research in the more comfortable environs of Bawdsey Manor. The *Jolly Sailor*'s beer is local, from Southwold; this is a recommendation.

At Southwold itself, or rather to the south of this most pleasant of seaside towns, is the *Harbour Inn*, near the mouth of the River Blyth. The Blyth Navigation, up to Halesworth through a tidal

staunch and four locks, opened to high hopes in 1761. After a few
years wherries became the regular craft using the navigation, trans-
shipping goods to coastal vessels a short way upstream from the
inn. But the entrance to the harbour always presented problems;
shoals came and went and came again and there was never enough
outflow from the river to clear them. Enclosure and reclamation of
the saltings at Blythburgh by self-seeking landowners reduced
greatly the flow of water available; entrance to the harbour became
increasingly difficult and sometimes impossible. The long and sad
story of the decay of the harbour and the consequent destruction of
the livings of the traders and watermen is told by Roy Clark in
Black Sailed Traders. The last wherry to use the navigation was the
Star, broken up in 1911 when her owner, F. G. Lambert, after a
long struggle gave up the cause as hopeless. In his reckoning the
Blyth Navigation even then could have been restored for £1,000,
but from nowhere was the money forthcoming.

The *Harbour Inn*, its beer also the excellent local product, is very
old, parts of it possibly dating from the fifteenth century. It is built
on a split level; the lower portion is frequently flooded, and some
of the locals can remember a dinghy tied up outside a bedroom
window. There is a flood level mark on the white-painted frontage.
Shallow draught boats can still use the river and plenty of them are
moored outside, many of them fishing boats. Inside the pub is a
collection of photographs of splendid faces rich in character, all
of them fishermen who were or are customers of the *Harbour Inn*.
There has been some tactful modernisation, but the beer is still
drawn from the wood. Of course it is said to have been a smugglers'
pub; but what pub along this coast was not?

At Halesworth, the other end of the old Navigation, the name of
the *Wherry Inn* is one of the few reminders of the waterborne trade.
But this is an early twentieth-century building, replacing the original *Wherry*, a thatched house unluckily destroyed by fire. The
basin a few yards away has been filled in and the maltings which
the wherries once served have been demolished. There is a fresh
water spring in the floor of the pub cellar, useful for keeping the
temperature down in summer. Visually, however, the pub's sign
showing a wherry under sail is the most attractive thing about it.

14

THE BROADS

∿∿∿∿∿∿∿∿∿∿∿∿∿∿∿∿∿∿∿∿∿∿∿∿∿∿∿∿∿

It is difficult, perhaps impossible, to define what makes a good pub, whether waterside or no. What is clear is that views differ, often quite violently. Perhaps nowhere do they differ more than in the Broads, where old inhabitants say that there is no longer a pub which they can go into with any pleasure, while crowded car-parks and moorings and bars packed solid with customers testify to the pleasure being found there by others. Years ago many of these pubs, isolated, perhaps miles from the nearest village, served only wherrymen and wildfowlers; today they are open to anybody who can afford to hire a boat or run a car. The big breweries have taken over; walls have been torn down, extensions run up; the old wooden settles are becoming as rare as wooden hulls on the Broads themselves. In the Broads as elsewhere it is not that people drink more but that there are simply more people; it is a sobering thought, in more ways than one, that a licensee may make nearly as much profit from juke-box and one-arm bandit as he does from the sale of beer.

Many Broads pubs stand at ferry crossings; although the ferries may no longer operate they endured long enough to enable the pub to make the transition to serving the pleasure trade. At Reedham the ferry still functions in the summer, being the only means of crossing the Yare between Yarmouth and Norwich. The *Ferry House Inn* housed the ferryman since the early seventeenth century; before then the Yare was forded but improvements to the river led to increase in depth. There were two more ferries above this point, but they ceased working during the war. The Reedham ferryman used to be responsible for the maintenance of the windmill, now inhabited but decapitated, one of three which drained this level.

The *Ferry House*, which has grown from a cottage about one-quarter of its present size, is a pleasant place with an interesting collection of old brewers' advertising material and bottles. It has had only three landlords in the past hundred years. Longevity here seems to have been the rule; Jeremiah Hoggett, in a copy of an affidavit preserved in the pub, states that he was the ferryman at the age of seventy-two and that his father had taken on the job in 1773. The tolls charged by his father had not been increased. They were as follows:

4 wheel vehicle	2s 6d (free return)
Gig	9d single
Donkey and cart	6d
Horse, donkey or mule, with rider	1½d
Sheep or pig	½d
Other animals	1d
Passengers	1d

Although at other Broads ferries a rowing boat is sometimes available, Reedham is the last of the old horse ferries still capable of ferrying a horse.

Above Reedham the *Beauchamp Arms* stands by the old ferry crossing at Buckenham and the *Coldham Hall* by the crossing to Brundall. *Coldham Hall* bears the date 1802 on a gable, but the red-brick house is probably older and may have been a shooting box at one time. There is a boat-building yard adjacent where wherries used to be repaired. This was very much a wherryman's pub. A previous landlord could recall being summoned by his father to see the last of the Norfolk keels sailing by about the year 1880. The square-rigged keels were familiar on the Broads until the mid-nineteenth century but were clumsy and slow compared to the Norfolk wherries which replaced them. These splendid vessels, with their long vanes and great single fore-and-aft sail, could point close to the wind and were as ideally suited to the conditions of Broads navigation as the 70ft narrow boat was to the Midlands canals. Four hours from Yarmouth to Norwich would have been a fair time in reasonable conditions. Today although there are several converted wherries to be seen there is only one left still under sail: *Albion*, built in 1898 and owned by the Norfolk Wherry Trust. *Albion* is not really typical, being carvel instead of clinker-built as was customary, but she is the last of the line of craft on which Broadland depended for the necessities of life.

Two of these necessities were handled at Surlingham, the next ferry crossing towards Norwich. Here was a coaling station for the neighbouring villages, and an old ice-house. Ice gathered from Surlingham Broad in the winter was stored here and then loaded into wherries which took it to the fish markets in Yarmouth. The *Ferry House Inn* dates from 1725 and began life as a court house where land disputes were argued. At one time it was owned by Lord Rosebery and it still comes under the lordship of the local manor. The building was enlarged, an extra gable being added in the nineteenth century, and paintings in the bar recall the scene a hundred years ago.

A few miles north of Surlingham, on the River Bure, is one of the best-known of Broads pubs, the *Ferry Inn* at Horning. There was a Roman station here, and the ferry itself may date back a thousand years. In the thirteenth century the name of the ferryman is recorded as being Gabbard; the ferry was on the route from Norwich to St Benet's Abbey, of which only fragmentary ruins remain, whose history stretched from the ninth to the sixteenth century, and was the burial place of Sir John Fastolfe. The present *Ferry Inn* is modern; its Georgian predecessor was destroyed in 1941 when three German bombs fell on and beside it. Several airmen enjoying an evening's relaxation were killed, and Douglas Bader escaped by only a few seconds. The chain ferry stopped working a few years ago, defeated by the attacks of pleasure

cruisers which rammed it frequently. The *Ferry Inn* was damaged
by fire in 1965, but was fortunate in its restorers and the building
does not disfigure the river bank. As at Surlingham, a painting in
the bar shows the scene as it was in the last century. There is one
other ferry pub on the Bure below Horning: the *Ferry Boat* at
Stokesby. This is good grazing country, and cattle used to be
ferried across here to the marshes on the southern side.

Between Horning and Stokesby, though nearer to the latter, is
one of the oldest inns on the Broads: the *Bridge* at Acle. This was
originally the guesthouse of Weybridge Priory, of which nothing
remains. Its earlier name as a pub was the *Angel*; W. A. Dutt refers
to it under this name in his classic book *The Norfolk Broads*, published 1903. He describes two brilliantly painted wherries moored
by the bridge, their colours 'reflected in the water, where they
shimmered and melted into one another whenever a breath of wind
or a passing boat sent ripples running towards the shore'. There
was a limekiln beside the pub, which was convenient for the working wherrymen. The *Bridge* now has a Kiln Bar with a thatched
roof, and it is an interesting exercise to distinguish the medieval
from the modern in various parts of the building. To confuse the
issue, the entrance door comes from a church at Burlingham. In the
days of the old bridge across the Bure at Acle the area was said to be
haunted by the ghosts of convicts hanged from the bridge itself
and uneasily seeking a more comfortable resting-place.

The head of navigation of the Bure for cruisers is Coltishall,
although until 1912 it was possible to penetrate to Aylsham if you
could manage the 3 locks and 7 bridges in the 11-mile stretch.
Dutt describes Coltishall as 'the most picturesque waterside village
in Broadland', and seventy years later many would think this claim
still holds true. It is very busy with visitors in the summer season
but has not suffered the architectural devastation that descended
upon Wroxham. The public staithe at Coltishall is in the guardian-
ship of the Broads Society; the *Rising Sun* faces downstream at the
end of the common. It is an attractive pink-washed two-storey
building which looks to have undergone little alteration apart from
the removing of interior dividing walls. A short distance downstream is the *Anchor*. This has been a pub for about 150 years. It
consists of two seventeenth-century Flemish weavers' cottages

with the courtyard between them built over when the conversion was done. The characteristic gables show the origin of the *Anchor*, and there are traces of otherwise inexplicable doorways here and there. Next to the *Anchor* is Clifford Allen's boatyard, one of the oldest on the Broads, into which an old malthouse has been incorporated. Mr Allen's great-grandfather bought the yard in 1864 and hired out his first boat a year later. Possibly this marked the beginning of what is now the Broads' major industry. Allen's also built the last of the trading wherries, *Ella*, in 1912, and the privately owned *Solace*, built about 1905, is moored here. Famous for traditional craftsmanship, Allen's yard is of major importance in the history of Broads navigation.

There are two interesting pubs on the northern edge of Broadland. It is inaccurate to describe the *Sutton Staithe Hotel* as a pub today, but it used to be the *Wherryman's Arms*, a rough old place at the end of Sutton Broad, an isolated beerhouse where brandy and gin smuggled in via Yarmouth were disposed of. Possibly some of it found its way to the Revd James Woodforde, whose diary records several illicit deals. Woodforde paid £1 18s for a tub of four gallons of brandy and £1 3s for the same quantity of gin, which he bottled as soon as possible. He also bought tea, expensive at up to 10s 6d a pound. It is said that the men in charge of the draining windmills warned the smuggling wherrymen of the presence of excisemen in the vicinity by setting their sails in a certain position, altering the setting to give the all clear. The *Wherryman's Arms* was closed down early in the nineteenth century and the building became a farmhouse. In 1928 it was reopened in its present form as a hotel, a comfortable red-brick place housing a fine collection of furniture and antiques.

Not far away by road, at the north end of Hickling Broad, is the *Pleasure Boat*. This was an old farmhouse, sold about 1880 to become a pub, taking its name from the type of wherry built specifically for pleasure boating. It was extended early this century in the same style, and recently has had a further extension to cope with the increased trade. Like Surlingham, this was a coaling station. The Broad was a seaplane base in World War I. But the great days of the *Pleasure Boat* must have been at the time when it first became a pub, as described by Oliver G. Ready in *Life and Sport on the Norfolk*

Broads, 1910, in which he remembers his boyhood and youth on the
Broads some 30 years earlier.

> It was a bright summer morning with hot sun and gusty westerly
> breeze. Unusual bustle had replaced the ordinarily trance-like
> quietude of the *Pleasure Boat Inn*.
>
> Without, three or four sedate-looking cobs, harnessed to high
> square carts and hitched to convenient gate posts, seemed almost
> to beat time with dull hoof thuds, in attempts to free their legs
> from the attentions of hungry flies.
>
> Within, the sound of loud, cheery voices, bursts of laughter,
> and the frequent rattle of pint-pots on bare wooden tables,
> denoted brisk business.
>
> But it was the narrow path leading to the front staithe that
> claimed every attention, for along its whole length lay boats of
> various sizes, shapes, colours and ages, all lateen rigged, with sails
> hoisted and flapping in the breeze, while aboard or on the path,
> men and youths with rolled-up sleeves were putting the finishing
> touches; a new lashing here, a block changed there, a few stitches
> in the leech to prevent quivering, and throwing up water on to the
> sails to make them hold the wind.
>
> It was Hickling water-frolic, and the first match was about to
> start. . . .
>
> On the staithe a troop of niggers provided music and much
> merriment, while the continuous roar of voices from the inn
> parlour proclaimed a busy day for the trade. . . .
>
> Next day we learned that more fights than usual had kept
> matters lively at the *Pleasure Boat* till a late hour, and as several of
> the gladiators had been 'pulled', water-frolic interest continued
> unabated till fitting pains and penalties had been inflicted by the
> local magistrate.

Accustomed, then, to water-frolics, the *Pleasure Boat* was clearly
able to cope with the unexpected visit of the Duke of Edinburgh
and Prince Charles when they were marooned there for two nights
in 1959 cut off from the house of their hosts by unpredicted floods.

Oliver Ready has a reminiscence of another Broadland pub, the
Berney Arms. He recalls a cold, damp day on the yacht *Zephyr*:

> Far away across that desolate waste of mud-flats was a tiny speck,
> the *Berney Arms Inn*, standing in lonesome dreariness on a marsh
> at the top of Breydon; but on that Sunday morning what a beacon
> of hope it was!
>
> We kept on saying: 'When we get to the *Berney Arms*'—we

would rest, have breakfast, lunch, get hot coffee. It was our longed-for haven.

Well, we got there about one o'clock, thoroughly exhausted, wet, cramped, and faint with hunger.

Hastily lowering sail and making *Zephyr* fast, we limped round a blank wall to the front entrance and saw . . . the door off its hinges and the windows all blown in. The place was abandoned!

Neither of us spoke as we crawled through the dank grass back to *Zephyr*.

Getting out some damp biscuits and pouring out some cold water, we broke our fast, still in silence.

The *Berney Arms*, having been a popular house for wherrymen who tied up there while waiting for the tide for Yarmouth, was indeed closed for many years, legend saying as a result of the drowning of three wherrymen in the river, but it is open again and callers today will get everything that Oliver Ready required. The well-known windmill, now an official historic monument, used to grind materials for a cement works as well as draining the marshes; it is likely that the real reason for the pub's closing was the shutting down of the cement works in 1880. Fortunately the reopening of the *Berney Arms* provides navigators again with the only safe mooring in the 9 miles between Reedham and Yarmouth.

The Bure, Ant, Yare and Waveney are the principal rivers of Broadland. The *Berney Arms* is near the confluence of Yare and Waveney. At one time navigation on the Waveney extended to Bungay; now the limit of navigation is the derelict Shipmeadow lock. On the north side, in Norfolk, are the Geldeston marshes; the Barsham marshes are on the south. Beside the lock is a little pub, known for over thirty years as 'Susan's' but licensed under its official name of *The Locks*. There is no road to *The Locks* and no other house nearby; access is by water or along a grassy track from Geldeston village over a mile away. There is no electricity, no gas, no running water; it is another world.

The Locks stands on an island. There was originally a mill on the site, about 300 years ago. When the lock was constructed, this part of the buildings became the lock cottage and a licence was granted. Not only wherry men used the pub; as the river forms the county boundary the marshes were a popular place for prize-fighting as it was only necessary to cross the river or the mill-stream to escape from the police of whichever county was more alert. Smugglers used the pub; so did wildfowlers, poachers and ghosts. So, in more recent years, did a host of people from all walks of life, drawn there by the unique character of the pub itself and the striking personality of its owner, Miss Susan.

The pub itself is very small, of whitewashed brick with a pantiled roof, two rooms up, two down. As you approach, you note that the track is reinforced by hundreds of crown corks trodden into the mud. There are two plank bridges to cross, and some vegetation to struggle through, before you arrive at the side of the house. There is no brewer's sign, only a small board over the front door: 'The Locks', Ellingham, Free House. Inside, you step a hundred years into the past. High-backed wooden settles line the room; there are highly polished old chairs and tables and a brick and iron fireplace and cooking stove, antique and complex. Paraffin lamps and candlesticks stand on every surface. You could not get draught beer ('you can get it in the village,' Susan used to say to customers she did not like the look of) because it was too difficult to roll the barrels from the track to the pub. But Susan was 'famous for her sherry.'

I have had to use the past tense. Miss Dorothy Ellis—Susan— died aged seventy-seven at the end of March 1973. She had kept *The Locks* for 35 years, at first in company with a gentleman whom all knew as 'Grumpy', but latterly alone. She had dignity, courage, humour and a mind very much of her own. If she did not like the look of you, you would not be encouraged to stay. If you confessed to being the driver of a car—even if you had left it a mile away at the head of the track—you were allowed only one glass of bottled beer. If you preferred tea, you could have it with pleasure; and if she knew it was your birthday she might bake you a cake. Susan's courage enabled her to take all in her stride: Black Shuck, the great dog that haunts the marshes, and the ghost of the seventeenth-century Flemish adventurer who once visited her parlour. One evening when the river was in flood a young couple drove down the track in a van and called at *The Locks*. One bottle of Guinness was all they were allowed, and they soon departed. Next morning Susan left to walk to the village and saw a dog sitting on what appeared to be a raft in the river. She looked more closely and described what seemed to be a pair of doors beneath the raft. Concluding that there appeared to be a van in the water, she continued to the village and informed the local constable. The van, the police discovered, belonged to the young couple, who had tried to turn it and had reversed into the river. Susan came back later, spent the evening as usual but could not sleep. At 4am she got up to light the fire and make some coffee. It was winter, pitch-black. There were no sticks in the house, so she groped her way to the woodshed. Her outstretched hand touched something unusual—something that should not be there. She went back to the house for a lamp and returned to the woodshed to find the bodies of her customers of the evening before, stretched out cold and clammy on a table. Mildly disconcerted because no one had told her they were there, she collected her sticks, lit the fire and made her coffee.

Although ill and unable to walk upstairs Susan continued to run *The Locks* until two weeks before her death. She was a fighter; she fought illness as she fought the River Authority, the Waveney itself—which at times forced her to retreat upstairs whence she would have to be rescued by boat—and the farmer who obstructed the track so that the beer lorry could not get through. She also fought commercialism, pretentiousness and vulgarity—and she won. She willed *The Locks* to a friend who had helped her, and after her death it was put up for auction. The site was described as 'giving considerable commercial and waterside potential,'—a phrase and an idea at which she would have shuddered. In the face of hot competition, the River Commissioners bought it for over £19,000, to ensure that the location would not be ruined by commercial development, and have given permission to Susan's old friend Walter to reopen the pub and run it in the traditional way. You may, of course, now have to pay for your drinks as you have them, instead of being presented with a bill at the end of the evening; you may be served, instead of going out to the cellar to serve yourself. You may no longer be presented with a key if you wish to use the lavatory, nor warned to bang on the door first to scare the rats away. But you will have the benefit of Walter's Norfolk humour and his fund of stories, many of which will tell you more about Susan, the 'Boadicea of the Broads'.

ACKNOWLEDGEMENTS

Without the help of a great many licensees and regulars of various public houses this book could not have been written, and I have pleasure in acknowledging my gratitude to them.

Others who helped by providing guidance and information include Messrs Alf Bailey, Guy Cliff, Walter Coe, Richard Dean, W. C. Fieldgate, Hugh Garrod, Mrs D. Hardcastle, Roger Hasdell, Reg Holmes, Alex Kinnear, A. F. Leach, G. J. Levine, Tony Lewery, T. Linfoot, R. W. Malster, J. P. Nelson, Lionel Munk, Miss Enid Porter, Adrian Russell, Philip Stevens. Jon H. Talbot and the Surrey & Hampshire Canal Society were most generous with information on the Basingstoke Canal and its pubs. Mrs Susan Farnell and Sir John Dunnington-Jefferson gave valuable information on the Derwent. Thanks also to J. L. Gilbert and Jim Yard.

I am grateful to several public libraries, especially Cambridge (Michael Petty), Goole and Wigan; to the Buckinghamshire and Warwickshire County Record Offices; to the Coventry *Evening Telegraph* and the East Anglian *Daily Times* for permission to use material; to the Ironbridge Gorge Museum Trust.

Mr A. T. E. Binsted of the Brewers' Society gave me useful help at the outset. Many brewers helped with lists of houses and other information, including especially Bass Charrington, Marston's, Watney Mann, Whitbread, Greene King, Mitchells & Butlers, Greenall Whitley, Ansell's, Wadworth's, Ind Coope and Guinness.

Photographs not credited were taken by myself. Messrs Stan Robertson, Jack Casselden and Peter Scott helped with the preparation of photographs. I hope Robert Cox's drawings give the reader as much pleasure as they do me.

The picture on the jacket is from a painting by Antony Warren. For permission to reproduce it I am indebted to him and to Miss Sheila Doeg of British Waterways Board, editor of *Waterways News*.

My final acknowledgement is to my wife Jill. Her ability to elicit information far outstrips my own and her persistence drove me on when all I wanted to do was fall asleep.

INDEX

(Pubs to which only passing reference is made are not included in the Index)

175